The Meiji Japanese Who Made Modern Taiwan

The Meiji Japanese Who Made Modern Taiwan

By Toshio Watanabe

Translated by Robert D. Eldridge

LEXINGTON BOOKS

Lanham • Boulder • New York • London

Published by Lexington Books
An imprint of The Rowman & Littlefield Publishing Group, Inc.
4501 Forbes Boulevard, Suite 200, Lanham, Maryland 20706
www.rowman.com

86-90 Paul Street, London EC2A 4NE

British Library Cataloguing in Publication Information Available

Library of Congress Cataloging-in-Publication Data

Names: Watanabe, Toshio, 1939- author. | Eldridge, Robert D., translator.
Title: The Meiji Japanese who made modern Taiwan / Toshio Watanabe ; translated by
    Robert D. Eldridge.
Other titles: Taiwan o Kizuita Meiji no Nihonjin. English
Description: Lanham : Lexington Books, [2022] | Includes bibliographical references and
    index. | Summary: "This book examines the policies and personalities behind Japan's
    administration of Taiwan from 1895 to 1945. The author examines various important
    figures that contributed to the development of modern Taiwan, such as Kodama
    Gentaro, Goto Shinpei, Hatta Yoichi, and others"—Provided by publisher.
Identifiers: LCCN 2021059724 (print) | LCCN 2021059725 (ebook) |
    ISBN 9781666908534 (cloth) | ISBN 9781666908558 (paperback) | ISBN
    9781666908541 (ebook)
Subjects: LCSH: Japanese—Taiwan—Biography. | Taiwan—Politics and
    government—1895-1945. | Taiwan—History—1895-1945 | Japan—Colonies—
    Taiwan—History—20th century. | Taiwan—Civilization—Japanese influences.
Classification: LCC DS799.72.A2 W36 2022 (print) | LCC DS799.72.A2 (ebook) |
    DDC 951.249/04—dc23/eng/20211221
LC record available at https://lccn.loc.gov/2021059724
LC ebook record available at https://lccn.loc.gov/2021059725

Contents

List of Figures

Translator's Preface

I first met the author, Watanabe Toshio, in the summer of 1997, when he attended a talk I, then a graduate student at Kobe University, gave at the PhD Kenkyukai, a study group for doctoral students and more senior scholars formed many years before, conducted at the International House of Japan in Tokyo. Over the years, we had a couple of other opportunities to meet, such as at the Masayoshi Ohira Memorial Foundation, which awarded one of my books (the Japanese version of *The Origins of U.S. Policy in the East China Sea Islands Dispute: Okinawa's Reversion and the Senkaku Islands*, 2014) its prestigious prize in 2016. Watanabe served on the committee judging the nominated books.

That same year, my professional involvement with Taiwan had begun with the opportunity to attend the inauguration of Dr. Tsai Ing-wen as president of Taiwan in May (2016). I subsequently learned that Professor Watanabe was also closely connected to Taiwan in his capacity as the chairperson, Friends of Lee Teng-hui Association in Japan, an organization of Japanese and Taiwanese supporters of the former president. (I myself joined in 2019, becoming, I think, the only American in it.)

Dr. Lee, a mentor of President Tsai and a former president himself, unfortunately passed away four months after the publication of the Japanese version of this book, *Taiwan o Kizuita Meiji no Nihonjin* (translated here as "The Meiji Japanese Who Made Taiwan"), but as an avid reader fluent in Japanese, he completed it before his passing at the age of ninety-seven.

By the time I met Professor Watanabe again at the aforementioned award ceremony for my book in June 2016, the first time in many years, he had recently stepped down as the chancellor of Takushoku University, a university founded in 1900 with strong connections to Taiwan, and had assumed the leadership of the Friends of the Lee Teng-hui Association in March 2016.[1] He continues to serve as an advisor to the university and publishes at an admirable pace, despite being eighty-two years old.

For example, a year after the Japanese version of this book came out, Watanabe released *Gotō Shinpei no Taiwan* ("Gotō Shinpei's Taiwan") in early 2021. He also helped to check this English version.

Prior to assuming the presidency of the university, he published an early edition of his memoirs, *Watashi no Naka no Ajia* ("The Asia in Me," 2004) which provides a fascinating overview of the evolution of political economy studies in Japan focusing on a developing Asia. He was at the center of these efforts.

Watanabe was born on June 22, 1939, in Yamanashi Prefecture, west of Tokyo. He attended Keio University, graduating with a B.A. in Economics in 1963. After working for a pharmaceutical company for two years, he returned to Keio University for graduate school. He completed the master's and doctoral courses there in 1967 and 1970, respectively. He received his Ph.D. in 1980.

He worked as a research assistant, lecturer, and associate professor at Kantō Gakuin University in Yokohama from 1967 to 1975 before joining Tsukuba University in Ibaraki Prefecture as an associate professor and later professor until 1989. After serving as a professor at Tokyo Industrial University for slightly more than a decade, he joined Takushoku University's Department of International Development in 2000, serving as its dean concurrently with being the director of the Institute for International Development, among other posts.

In 2005, he was chosen as the president of Takushoku University, as well as of its graduate schools, serving in this capacity for eight years. During the last two years of his second term, he was also appointed the chancellor of the school, with his term in that latter capacity extending until 2015 as mentioned earlier.

In addition to his academic positions, he has also given to the profession by holding the chairmanship or senior positions in several academic associations related to his specialties of international development and the political economy of Asia. Watanabe has contributed to the community by serving on a number of government councils and on the boards of a number of foundations and think tanks.

Watanabe's academic specialization is development economics, with a focus on the economies of Asia. He began his research examining the South Korean economy, conducting fieldwork there and assisting the Institute of Developing Economies as a junior researcher. His publications attracted much attention for his path-breaking research and unique insights, and before long, he was honored with a number of prestigious academic awards. He was invited to serve on numerous government committees, including that examining official development assistance, and was an active participant in academic associations and international exchange.

Taiwan was one of the countries he examined too with its being one of the four "Economic Tigers"—also known as the "Asian Tigers" or "Asian Dragons." After South Korea and Taiwan, the other two were Singapore and Hong Kong. Each transformed their economy from low income to advanced economies in just a few decades.

Watanabe was at the forefront of this research. The more he examined these economies, the more he became interested in their histories. In particular, he was very interested in Japan's involvement with the development of modern Taiwan, from 1895 to 1945, when Japan administered the island. It was only in recent years that he had the time to write about this history.

He wrote the book you have before you in an effort to explain how Japan's truly "best and brightest" gave their all to help develop Taiwan. The book is divided into ten chapters, including this Introduction, and Conclusion, as well as a Translator's Preface to the English Version. The last two chapters, chapter 7 and the Conclusion, discuss the importance of Japan's administration of Taiwan in an international context. The Conclusion also compares why the administration of Taiwan is considered so successful and Taiwanese most grateful, while Koreans harbor resentment toward Japan for its administration.

As I am very interested in Taiwan-Japan relations and recognized the importance of having this work available in English, I immediately contacted Professor Watanabe about translating the book. He readily agreed.

Other than ensuring a greater use of footnotes, I did not make any significant changes to the book. The reader will notice that the chapters are not necessarily in chronological order. On the surface, it might make more sense to restructure the chapters in order to make them read more chronologically, but most of the chapters span long periods themselves, and are intertwined with the other chapters, so I felt it was unnecessary in the end to change up the order.

I thank Professor Watanabe with entrusting me with this important work and for answering my many questions along the way. I am grateful to Professor Watanabe's able assistant, Ishizaki Rie, who helped with many different tasks during this project—too numerous to count. My wife, Emiko, and children (now adults), Ami and Kennan, as always provided much support and love during the project.

I also thank the team at Lexington Books for their assistance with the publication of the book. I began publishing with them almost twenty years ago and continue to be impressed with their dedication and professionalism.

On a final note, with Dr. Watanabe's permission, I dedicate the English version of this book to Mr. Tsujii Masafusa, vice chairperson of the Friends of Lee Teng-hui Association and a strong supporter of Taiwan in Japan. I have the pleasure of knowing him for more than fifteen years, the last five years in connection with Taiwan. My life in the Kansai region of Japan has been enriched by his presence here, as has my understanding of Japan-Taiwan relations.

Robert D. Eldridge, PhD
July 2021
Kobe, Japan

NOTE

1. Takushoku University was established as the Taiwan Association School (*Taiwan Kyōkai Gakkō*) to produce graduates who could contribute to the development of Taiwan. In 1918, it changed its name to Takushoku, which means "development" and "industrialization," as well as colonization.

Introduction

"My resting for one day means Japan's modernization will be delayed an extra day."

This was how Furuichi Kōi responded when the female proprietor of the boarding house at which he lived during his time abroad studying in Paris suggested that he take the day off. Seeing him constantly studying, she had become worried about his health. During the night, feverish, he had been crying out in his sleep, but that morning he was up preparing to go to the university.

Furuichi had been put in charge of the construction along the Shinano River, flowing through Nagano and Niigata Prefectures to the Sea of Japan, and Agano River, originating in Fukushima and Gunma Prefectures and flowing through Niigata Prefecture to the same sea, which heralded in the dawn of the engineering fields of river and port construction. If Japan did not quickly learn Western civilization and become a modern and independent nation, it would not be able to exist as a civilized state. Furuichi was at the forefront of learning Western technology, being sent overseas at government expense. He did not have the luxury of worrying over a fever.

This episode at the boarding house epitomizes the intense patriotism and sense of mission and honor among the Meiji technical experts and engineers. Furuichi later became the first president of the Imperial College of Engineering which was the forerunner of Tokyo University's Faculty of Engineering. One of his students, Hiroi Isami, is known as the engineer who built the breakwaters at Otaru Port, which faced the strong winter winds, in Hokkaido. He succeeded Furuichi to become a professor at the Imperial College and himself inspired many students. These students were precious to Japan, modernizing as it was at the time, helping to further the field of civil engineering.

Aoyama Akira, a disciple of Hiroi, decided to help with the construction of the Panama Canal upon graduation and traveled by himself to the site, an area rampant with tropical diseases, to work. He demonstrated his ability and was made a surveyor. Upon returning to Japan, Aoyama was entrusted with an extremely difficult construction job, the so-called Shinano Okōzu Channel Project, which would divide the Shinano River in Niigata Prefecture to reduce the risk of downstream flooding by adding what was then called the New Shinano River (and is now known as the Okōzu Channel). The inscription on the monument to commemorate the start of the construction alongside the river reads, simply and beautifully, "For humanity, for our country."

Hatta Yoichi, who revered his teacher Hiroi and his senior Aoyama, graduated from the Imperial College of Engineering in 1910. Upon completion of his studies, he immediately left, without hesitation, for the unexplored frontier of Taiwan, becoming an engineer in the Civil Engineering Department of the governor-general's office, the de facto central authority for the colonial administration of Taiwan.

The Tropic of Cancer goes through the central part of Taiwan. Above it, the north has a subtropical and temperate climate, and below it, the south belongs to a tropical climate with regular monsoons. The Chiayi-Tainan Plain (hereafter, Chianan Plain) is suited for growing rice. However, when Hatta first visited the 2,500 km^2 alluvial plain, it was simply comprised of rain-fed paddy fields. It seemed as if the harvest each time—whether it was good, bad, or famine-like—was based on the Heavens. Human effort seemed to have no effect on the outcome. During the dry season, the soil lost moisture and became hard, and even plows did not work. Because of the Central Mountain Range running north to south like a spine through Taiwan, during the rainy season, most of the water rushes from the steep mountains down to the plains in torrents, flooding the plains and burying the rice fields. The development of the Chianan Plain meant water irrigation facilities controlling water during the rainy season and providing water during the dry season.

Back in Japan proper, the lack of rice was particularly severe on the eve of the Russo-Japanese War (1904–1905), and there were frequent rice riots around the country. The leadership of the governor-general's office in Taiwan, who had long heard about Hatta's concept to develop the Chianan Plain, directed him to go ahead with it as it would help alleviate the rice crisis, as well as contribute to the financial independence of Taiwan. Hatta's vision was truly grand. By building a dam (which became the Wushantou Dam) at this location, water could be stored and then released to the plain area in a controlled manner. Moreover, in order to acquire more water when the reservoir was low, a tunnel of more than 3,000 meters was dug to divert water from the Zengwen River to the Wushantou Reservoir. The volume of water released could encircle half the diameter of the earth. As such, the bleak plain became a carpet of green.

Hatta's vision was seen not only in the "hard" areas, such as the dam construction method, but in the "soft" area of employing the "Three-Field System" used by farmers in Europe of the Middle Ages. All his efforts were the result of hard, untiring work from beginning to end.

Speaking of untiring work, the development of the Formosan (hereafter, Hōrai) Rice variety took approximately twenty years, thanks to the efforts of Iso Eikchi. Iso graduated from the Tōhoku Imperial College of Agriculture (now Hokkaidō University's School of Agriculture) and arrived in Taiwan to work for the governor-general's office well after Hatta, in 1912. He was to address the problem of the lack of rice, the staple food for the colony.

Making a better variety of rice was a monotonous assignment, requiring continuous experimentation. Pollen with particularly good and special characteristics would be attached to equally special and very good quality pistils, the ovule-bearing organ of a seed plant, to mate them artificially, producing an even higher quality new variety. However, achieving success was difficult.

The efforts proved extremely disappointing, with no hope for a breakthrough in sight. An ordinary man would have given up, but Iso had an extraordinary amount of patience and perseverance. As a result, he succeeded in developing the Hōrai Rice variety as a unit crop of extremely high quality, and Taiwan was able to help the Japanese mainland with its original problem of the shortage of rice.

Both Hatta and Iso were born in 1886. Both were elites, trained at Imperial universities, and engineers. What prodded them was likely their sense of carrying out their duty as engineers.

The late novelist Shiba Ryōtarō wrote about Akiyama Yoshifuru, who graduated from the Imperial Army College in 1885 and became a captain in the calvary the following year, that

> a military man's duty is to defeat enemies of the country by becoming stronger as a soldier and prepared to do battle at any time . . . Everything else is irrelevant. If you think of these other things that are not important, you risk losing your concentration and focus.[1]

These two Japanese men, Hatta and Iso, epitomized this spirit. They worked hard as elite engineers in the administration of Taiwan and came to represent the ideal of Meiji Japan (1867–1912), the period when Japan itself was modernizing and gaining an honored place in the world.

Iso's Hōrai Rice was further improved later and introduced into all parts of Asia which had long struggled with the inability to feed rapidly growing populations with small-scale farming, triggering a "Green Revolution" in these areas. If this revolution had not taken place, Asia would likely have faced famine and starvation, such as that seen in North Korea in recent years.

One Japanese, who has since been forgotten but is discussed in this book, was greatly concerned about the lack of food in the Punjab region of India and worked to solve the problem. With the help of Iso and the government of the Republic of China, Sugiyama Tatsumaru introduced Hōrai Rice into the region, wracked by visible starvation everywhere, eventually saving it from starvation.

Sugiyama, who can be described (a little clumsily) as a "Shōwa Era [1926–1989] Person of Meiji," was the son of the mystery writer Yumeno Kyūsaku. He was also the grandson of the tactician Sugiyama Shigemaru, who exercised behind-the-scenes influence on some of the important ventures of Meiji Japan between the political and financial worlds.

This book begins by introducing the history of the development of Hōrai Rice by Iso as an epoch-making improved variety rice that led to Asia's "Green Revolution." It then traces the introduction of Hōrai Rice into the Punjab region by Sugiyama. Furthermore, this book looks at the challenges Hatta had with developing the Wushantou Dam necessary to produce Hōrai Rice in the first place. Despite the different fields and eras, their stories, in other words, are intertwined.

The book next discusses what the existence of Taiwan has meant to modern Japan. In particular, it looks at the fourth governor-general of Taiwan, Kodama Gentarō, an Imperial Japanese Army general and administrator, who later served as the chief of the general staff of the army in Manchuria during the Russo-Japanese War and helped to lead Japan to victory in that capacity. The book also looks at Gotō Shinpei, whom Kodama had asked to join him in Taiwan as the head of the civil affairs department of the administration, made significant contributions to Taiwan's modernization. By examining the thinking and actions of these two men, this book highlights the reasoning and boldness of the leaders of Meiji Japan (1868–1912) in order to help us better understand the spirit of the Meiji Japanese who lived in and worked on behalf of Taiwan and Japan.

NOTE

1. Shiba Ryōtarō, *Saka no Ue no Kumo*, Vol. 1 (Tokyo: Bungei Shunjū, 1999). The English version of this best-selling novel about the Russo-Japanese War, originally serialized between 1968 and 1972, was translated by Juliet Winters Carpenter and Paul McCarthy (edited by Phyllis Birnbaum) and was published by Routledge as *Clouds Above the Hill* in 2013.

Chapter 1

Iso Eikichi, the Father of Agriculture in Taiwan

"I HAVE THE RESPONSIBILITY TO FINISH MY WORK WITH HŌRAI RICE"

Iso Eikichi's postwar began in August 1945 with his reading of the Imperial Rescript on Surrender to his Japanese staff of the governor-general's office in Taiwan involved with the development of agriculture there. Speaking with tears rolling down his cheeks, Iso said at the end that the situation had worsened, and it would be necessary for them to carry on and contribute to the rebuilding of their country. He could barely get the words out.

Staying in Taiwan, Iso had to find ways to provide for his staff, prepare for their return to Japan, and protect the equipment and other materials in the related buildings and facilities of the governor-general's office. Sometimes, Iso himself would have to stand guard at night. He was busy doing many things unrelated to his work as an agriculture specialist.

No sooner had he completed the repatriation of his staff and breathed a sigh of relief that his wife, Tatsu, died suddenly of an illness. Decades before, the two were married in Sapporo, Hokkaido, with Iso's mentor from the Tōhoku Imperial College of Agriculture, Professor Niijima Yoshinao, having been the matchmaker. They moved to Taiwan right after the wedding. Tatsu never had the chance to return to Japan during that time, instead completely supporting her husband in his research, including making clean handwritten copies of all his rough drafts.

Even Tatsu, however, felt the desire to return to Japan when she saw all her close friends in Taiwan being repatriated. She begged Iso for them to return to Japan as well, but he told her he had to complete the work he started with Hōrai Rice even if the times had changed.

Figure 1.1   Iso Eikichi in his Office at National Taiwan University. *Source*: (from NTU website).

He tried to convince her in this way but, after more than forty years there, she desperately wanted to see Japan again. In response, he told her he understood and that he would get a travel bag for her so she could be ready to depart as soon as was possible. He explained he would buy one within the next few days and for her to put everything she thought she would need in it.

With this small hope in her heart, after Tatsu saw him off, she collapsed in the entranceway. Their younger daughter, Yuriko, who was still living at home with them, laid her mother down on a futon in the living room. She then telephoned her father who rushed home by car. Although a doctor came to check on her, he said she had a cerebral hemorrhage and could not be helped. There was nothing else that could be done, the doctor said, other than to watch her condition. Some twenty hours later, she opened her vacant eyes and without saying anything pointed upward several times. She may have been thinking of the scenery in her hometown of Sapporo.

Her husband whispered into her ear for her to go ahead of him and that he would eventually follow. She closed her eyes again, never to wake up. She passed away a week later. Iso put the unused travel bag he got for her in her casket.

All their close Japanese friends had since returned to Japan. A private funeral was conducted in Taiwan, which no longer belonged to Japan by this point. Tatsu, who had been a teacher at Hokusei Girls School in Sapporo before they were married, was Christian. However, Iso did not have the luxury to have a Christian funeral conducted for her, and instead had a simple one done in the Taiwanese style.

Iso would spend a total of twelve more years in Taiwan following the end of the war. During this time, he would answer questions from agriculture officials from the government of the Republic of China which wanted to expand production of Hōrai Rice and occasionally go out to the countryside to assist with its introduction using his already proven methods to instruct them.

Iso's doctoral dissertation, submitted to the Tōhoku (Taipei) Imperial University, introduced the birth of Hōrai Rice, but it did not include the development of later quality varieties, such as "Kagiban 2 Gō," "Taichū 65 Gō," and others. As such, Iso rewrote his doctoral dissertation in order to leave a book on plant breeding for the next generation based on his latest research. He moved his office from the Taichung Agricultural Experimentation Station to the School of Agriculture at Taipei Imperial University, where he had been given an office and called it "Iso's Hut." There he concentrated on publishing his findings in English. Subsequently, his work appeared as a UN Food and Agriculture Organization report in October 1954 entitled *Rice and Crops in its Rotation in Subtropical Zones.*

It was clear that the production of Hōrai Rice was important to Taiwan even under the new administration of the government of the Republic of China. This is seen by Iso's inclusion, in his essay ("Memories of Hōrai Rice"), of the lyrics of a song titled "Hōrai Rice is Delicious" that had been made by the Food Department of the ROC's Taiwan Province. This is particularly important because the government of the Republic of China, which had fled the mainland to Taiwan in 1949, spent many years seeking to destroy the legacy of Japan's administration of Taiwan and yet one of the government's departments prepared a song that inspired the farmers of the country. This suggested just how much Iso was loved and esteemed by Taiwan's farmers.

The song went as follows:

1. The rays of sunlight reach the green rice plants blowing in the breeze,
Suggest it will be a rich harvest,
This rice will certainly be tasty,
Its name: Taiwan's Hōrai Rice
Hōrai Rice, both delicious and good.

2. The gold-colored rice plants waving in the wind,
Cutting the rice plants with the young maiden farmgirls
Little birds chirp on the small mountain made of chaff
Its name: Taiwan's Hōrai Rice
Hōrai Rice, both delicious and good.

3. Taiwan has become a rice-producing island.
Both old and young dance over the bountiful year.
The people will have a prosperous century.
Hōrai Rice, acquainted with the stars.
Hōrai Rice, a treasured brand.[1]

THE RICE RIOTS THAT BECAME THE STIMULUS

In its improved form, Hōrai Rice became the product to generate a high income and promote the Taiwan brand around the world. It was the result of twenty years of effort and hard work.

At the time Iso joined the governor-general's office in Taiwan as an assistant engineer in March 1912, having graduated from the agricultural college in Sendai the previous year, there were said to have been at least 1,197 varieties of rice. In fact, prior to that, there were probably more than that but the farmers over time had likely done away with the varieties that were not appropriate, and thus this number was reached. But even then, 1,200 was an extremely large number. Iso was assigned to the Arboriculture Division of the Agricultural Experimentation Station in Taihoku (hereafter, Taipei), and there his job was to choose 390 varieties out of this initial 1,200 to see which fit Taiwan's conditions, and then select the best 175 out of those.

Two years before Iso came to Taiwan, Suenaga Megumu had arrived in 1910 also to look at improving the rice varieties there. Suenaga was a graduate of the Mie Agricultural School—the predecessor of the Mie Agricultural High School—in Oita Prefecture and served as an assistant engineer at the governor-general's office as well having worked previously at the Fukuoka Prefectural government's agricultural experimentation station. As assistant engineers, Suenaga and Iso would help the more senior engineers.

When Suenaga arrived at the Kagi (hereafter, "Chiayi," based on the modern name) Farm in 1910, the governor-general's office had just started that year with developing improved rice using that type found in Taiwan. The governor-general's office had hired an additional 300 graduates of the top agricultural schools in Japan assigning them to locations all around Taiwan. Suenaga was one of them.

Japan joined the Industrial Revolution around the time of the Sino-Japanese War (1894–1895) as the country urbanized and industrialized. Production of raw silk, cotton, shipbuilding, iron, coal, and so forth increased, and the labor force supporting this flowed from the farms and villages to the cities. Because of this, the labor force in rural areas, which produced the food, decreased, while the demand for food for the growing number of urban residents rapidly increased. As a result, Japan's food shortage became quite severe.

The bad harvest of 1889 caused rice prices to soar the following year. In January 1890, disgruntled, struggling people in Toyama Prefecture created a disturbance, and between April and August, this disquieting situation was repeated in other cities around the country, such as in Tottori, Niigata, Shimonoseki, and Takaoka. In Aikawa, on the island of Sado off Niigata Prefecture, some 2,000 miners rioted, with the Imperial Japanese Army being called in to try to quell the dispute. The disturbances continued, however, with the flames spreading to Fukui, Ehime, and Miyagi Prefectures as well.

The political unrest in various villages due to rice shortages did not end until the mid-1890s. Unfortunately, damage to the crops by storms and floods, not to mention that by disease and insects, occurred continuously at this time of year. The degree of poverty among the farming villages in Nagano, Toyama, Yamagata, Niigata, and other prefectures was particularly severe. For example, three years after the start of the Sino-Japanese War, which began in 1894, the situation had actually worsened.

If one set the rice production index at 100 for 1894, by 1897, it was below 90. It was still bad as Japan entered the Russo-Japanese War in 1904. Nevertheless, in February that year, the Imperial Rescript declaring war on Russia was issued, even though a country should not go to war when its most important supply—food—is lacking due to poor crops and bad harvests. Such a war is unsustainable over the long run.

In December 1901, the *Genrō*, or elder statesmen of the Meiji Era, comprising Yamagata Aritomo, Saigō Tsugumichi, Inoue Kaoru, Ōyama Iwao, and Matsukata Masayoshi, were joined by the newer members like Katsura Tarō (founder of the school that became Takushoku University), Komura Jutarō, Yamamoto Gonnohyōe, and others, where they firmed up their intention to form an alliance with England in order to prepare for war with Russia. The decision to go to war with Russia was approved at a June 1903 Imperial Conference, leading to the issuing of the Imperial Rescript declaring war on February 10, 1904.

The heavy chemical industry, which supports the munitions industry and employment, had been greatly strengthened during this time. The outflow of the working population from the farms and villages to the cities continued to grow, and the securing of food for the growing number of urban workers and increasing number of conscripted soldiers and sailors in the military became increasingly difficult. It essentially was impossible to cover this demand for rice, which grew exponentially, simply by rice production in Japan alone.

Thus, the expansion of the supply of rice in the recently ceded Taiwan became indispensable. The first three heads of the military government in Taiwan—Kabayama Sukenori, Katsura, and Nogi Maresuke—put their efforts into promoting the internal stability of Taiwan by suppressing the resistance of the residents by force. It was around the time that IJA Lieutenant General

Kodama Gentarō was assigned to become the fourth governor-general when the full-fledged development of Taiwan began. Kodama arrived in his post in February 1898 and was joined by the bureaucrat politician Gotō Shinpei who subsequently skillfully promoted the modernization of Taiwan as the director (later director-general) of civil administration.[2]

Kodama had Gotō conduct a thorough investigation of the land and population overall of Taiwan after arriving in his position and examined the current situation of Taiwan, whose management he was entrusted. Based on these investigations, Kodama invited influential people from Japan and Taiwan to gather at the governor-general's residence in November 1889 where he introduced the policy for the industrial development in Taiwan.

THE ORDER TO MODERNIZE
TAIWAN'S AGRICULTURE

After Taiwan became a part of Japan, arable land, water use facilities, and cultivated areas were expanded and improvements in rice varieties and inspections were introduced. These were not done on an individual, local trial-and-error basis, but rather part of a larger policy of the governor-general's office that Kodama had called for. This order became the turning point for Taiwan's agricultural modernization. The essence of the instruction was as follows.

The production of rice in Taiwan is the most important issue at present. However, although these spacious rice fields are blessed with a wonderful climate, the yield is not as large as the land area, and the quality of the rice is poor because the water supply is still not sufficiently developed. It is as if farmers do not consider rice cultivation as their vocation, but rather throw away the blessings bestowed upon them. If we could improve the water supply and cultivate the land properly, it would not be difficult to triple the current harvest. If this were to happen, the people of Taiwan would be able to eat three meals a day, and the surplus could be exported. Certainly, rice should be the mainstay of Taiwan's trade.[3]

What was in Kodama's heart at the time was the realization that if this large effort was not successful, that Japan's ability to win in the Russo-Japanese War was in doubt. It was a bold, but potentially highly risky decision.

Taiwan's rice production at the time met the island's internal demand. Taiwan was also able to export rice to mainland China, primarily to Fukien Province, across the Taiwan Strait. It would seem to have been easy to send the excess rice to Japan, but in fact, the rice grown in Taiwan did not match the Japanese diet whatsoever. There was a lot of so-called red rice, which had changed color due to the lack of nutrition in the soil and development.

Moreover, it was the simple, long grain Indica variety of rice, which was dry and not sticky like the Japanese kind. In contrast, the type of rice traditionally enjoyed in Japan was called the Japonica variety. It was rich in flavor, round, glutinous, and moist. If the Indica variety were shipped to Japan, it would likely have to be treated as third-class rice and sold at a low price because demand would be low as it did not suit Japanese tastes.

BEING IMPRESSED BY THE RESEARCH
OF SUENAGA MEGUMU

Interest in improving the rice variety grew in the second decade of the 1900s. Nineteen-ten, the year Suenaga arrived as an assistant engineer at the Chiayi Farm, was also the time that the governor-general's office had released the plans to improve the rice variety. The governor-general's office had instructed the Chiayi Agency Agricultural Association to choose the best rice variety whose grain was round like that found in rice from Japan, designate a special area to promote the cultivation of it, and plan to choose what was clearly the best variety to make a pure-strand line of it. In addition, they were to try to plant this variety in multiple locations and further spread the best variety of it.

This effort ended up achieving quite good results. The native type of rice, which had numbered 1,365 varieties, was narrowed down to 485 varieties before the activity. The native rice type began to advance toward unification.

However, this result was still far from complete for Suenaga. He knew that even if the native variety spread, there was still the question of the strong antipathy toward this type of rice in Japan proper. Suenaga understood shortly after he arrived that the only way to succeed was to improve upon the Japanese variety of rice and introduce it into Taiwan rather than trying to do anymore to improve the native type of rice.

In fact, Suenaga's essay, "A Humble Opinion about the Improvement of Rice by the Agency," that he wrote for a contest sponsored by the Chiayi Agency Agricultural Association for its engineers, was the only one among 270 entries to win top honors. Suenaga boldly argued that, although there was more experimentation to be done at the Chiayi Farm, there was more chance for success by improving on the Japanese variety than the local variety. His paper was a direct challenge to the official policy of the governor-general's office's to improve upon the local variety.

Success is not guaranteed when conducting selective breeding to improve the quality. There is an unlimited number of trial and error that one has to go through, with no end in sight. One might succeed, but even then, it is often by chance. It is because of these difficult experiments that the engineer who succeeds is given much fame and honor as a result of his or her labors.

As was mentioned in the Introduction, improving the quality of the rice plant involves attaching pollen with very good, special characteristics to high good quality pistils, the ovule-bearing organ of a seed plant, mating them artificially to produce an even higher quality new variety.

Unit crop refers to the amount that can be harvested in a unit area, such as one hectare. The most important criterion for a good variety is for the unit crop to be high. If the rice plant has fallen over, it is likely that the unit crop will not be high. As such, it is important for the stalk of the rice plant to be thick, and the height to be short so that it does not easily fall over.

It is also very important for there to be a high unit crop that photosynthesis occurs by getting the plant to stand as straight as possible. Similarly, it is important that each rice plant has many ears so that as many grains of rice as possible can be grown. Moreover, it is necessary that the rice plant be strong to be able to resist neck-rot and other diseases, while being tasty to suit the palates of the consumers, among other conditions when improving the rice variety.

It is said that in fact there are as much as ten conditions that must be met. If that is true, there would be about 1,000 varieties that would be artificially bred, with the best among them chosen. These would further be carefully selected based on the soil and climate conditions. This would have to be repeated constantly. Moreover, to check the results of the cultivation, the first crop would take one year, and the second one about four months. It could take forever to successfully improve the variety.

When seeking to improve the rice variety in this case, or other crops, it is sometimes necessary to completely get rid of preconceived notions and adopt pragmatism. Suenaga believed in this and as such made great strides in that direction.

Iso Eikichi was another one who was a complete believer in pragmatism. The contents of Suenaga's paper became known to Iso, who was working at the agricultural experimentation station in Bunbu Township near the governor-general's office.[4] At the experimental station there in Taipei, Iso selected a limited variety of native rice, seeking to improve on them. However, at the same time, he also experimented with seeking to improve upon the Japanese rice varieties. While he had yet to reach a determination, he increasingly recognized the superiority of Japanese rice. As a result, Iso became enamored with Suenaga's research.

In February 1914, the Chiayi Agency Agricultural Association sponsored another essay and presentation contest. Suenaga again won the first prize, having submitted two papers, among the 335 works entered. His two were entitled, "The Actual State of the Management of Chiayi Farm" and "A Humble Opinion on the Agricultural Policies of the Chiayi Agency." Both concluded that "Japanese rice variety was best for the Agency and it should in the future promote it."[5]

Two years after receiving the first prize, Suenaga was able to persevere in the breeding experiments using the Japanese rice variety, achieving the conclusion he had originally identified. This was well received and led to his becoming a key member of the Chiayi Agency Agricultural Association.

THE STRUGGLE TO DEVELOP HŌRAI RICE

Iso, who believed that the Taichung area of central Taiwan was better suited to grow rice than the Taipei area of northern Taiwan, asked the governor-general's office for a transfer to the Taichung Agricultural Experimental Station, one year after the second contest, in 1915. His wish was granted. Knowing Suenaga to be an excellent researcher, he asked that Suenaga also be transferred there. In light of their excellent collaboration together in practical researcher, later, the two became known as the "father and mother of Hōrai Rice." Upon his transfer, Iso went from assistant engineer to full engineer, becoming Suenaga's supervisor.

Taichung was a city built toward the end of the Meiji Era as a central western core city based on urban planning by the governor-general's office. The Taichung Railway Station, on what is now the Western Trunk Line, is a heavy brick building decorated in the Baroque style. A number of roads radiate from this station, and the nearby shopping streets tend to be filled with people. The clear Ryoku and Ryū rivers, alongside which willow trees were planted, flow through the central part of the city. To the east of the station is a parade ground and next to that is a source for the good quality water provided to the city. The water that is pumped up flows naturally and gracefully down the structures in place.

The Taichung Agricultural Experimental Station was situated in Shinko Town, one of the best maintained areas of Taichung. Approximately thirty people worked there. Suenaga visited the office, with its large roof, at the experimental farm and talked with Iso then for the first time.

Suenaga introduced himself, explaining he had been transferred from Chiayi Farm to the Taichung Agricultural Experimentation Station. He asked for Iso's support and guidance. As he did this, he bowed his head. Iso responded by thanking him for coming so quickly. He told him he had seen him at the second essay contest but apologized for not introducing himself at that time. He explained it had re-read Suenaga's paper, telling him it was "very convincing."[6]

Suenaga humbly responded that it was nothing great and that he still had a long way to go. Iso invited him to sit down on the sofa near his desk. Suenaga had read Iso's theoretical writings on breeding and was deeply impressed with them. He knew that Iso was one of the very best graduates of Tōhoku Imperial Agricultural College to be assigned to Taiwan.

Although Iso was just shy of thirty years old, his hair was already thinning, and he had the air of a more senior scholar. He had a gentle face and seemed to never lose his smile. Suenaga was relieved. He could hardly believe that they were the same age, having both been born in 1886.

Iso said he wanted to work together on the improvement of the Japanese variety of rice. The governor-general's office's policy was to pursue improvements on the native variety of rice, but at least it did not forbid experiments with the Japanese variety, he explained, reaching across the coffee table to shake Suenaga's hand. Accustomed more to the Japanese custom of bowing, Suenaga leaned in erect from the waist while extending his hand.

Iso would become greatly astonished by Suenaga's efforts at improving the quality of the rice in the farm fields at the Taichung Agricultural Experimentation Station. He would get up at 5.00 a.m. and travel four kilometers to work carrying the morning and lunch time obento boxes his wife Kuni made for him. He would leave for home around 7.00 p.m. or 8.00 p.m. and look at the morning paper over dinner. After that, he would go to Iso's home and report on the results of that day. They had so much to discuss that quite often he would not get home until after midnight, having lost track of time talking about the possibilities for improvements.

Suenaga told his wife that he felt as if he had been born to work with rice. He never sat still when he talked about it, nor did he take a day off. He did not even really need shoes, as he was always knee deep in the rice paddies.

However, the main focus of his work at the experimental station had to be in line with the policy of governor-general's office, namely the improvement of native varieties. Thanks to the efforts of the staff at the experimental station, they were able to specify the type of local grain which they artificially mated and transferred to the station's farm fields and repeated their testing there countless times. However, they were unable to overcome the limitations of that breed.

Concurrently, they sought to mate local rice varieties with Japanese rice strains, but they were unable to get the results they were looking for out of those trials. They produced 110 new varieties, but none of them was close to the round shape of Japonica rice. At times, they came close to succeeding, but it did not last long. Suenaga continued to grope in the dark for the right mix.

UNEXPECTED GROWTH OF THE JAPANESE VARIETY

The improvement of the Japanese variety was difficult, in the end, probably because Taiwan's soil and weather conditions were different compared to Japan, which is a long, narrow country running north to south with cold climates and subtropical ones. It was thus necessary to try different ways to help the plants grow, but even then, they were unsuccessful in getting any significant growth. What's more, sometimes, an insect disease would wipe out the whole crop.

With this, the idea emerged to find soil and weather conditions similar to Japan and try growing the Japanese variety of rice there.

Iso had worked at the Taipei Agricultural Experiment Station before he came to Taichung. At that time, Iso belonged to the Taipei Mountain Climbing Club which the staff in the governor-general's office who liked hiking and mountain climbing had formed. He looked for highlands that were similar to Japan's climate, hiking at Mt. Datun, Seven-Star (Qixing) Mountain, Mt. Guanyin, and Lake Zhuzi, all near Taipei.

When Iso explored the area around Lake Zhuzi, he felt that it was very similar to the dirt and climate of Kyushu in Japan. The lake had been formed by the volcanic activity in the past which had blocked rivers and streams. At an elevation of 600m, it was pleasantly cooler than the plains at sea level. The temperature was low, with an adequate amount of rainfall and rich soil. Moreover, the area is surrounded by mountains, which makes it difficult for outside varieties to naturally mate and disease to strike.

In addition to Lake Zhuzi, Iso chose other highlands such as Tamsui, Jinbaoli, and Keelung as strong candidates, and after getting the help of the Taipei Agricultural Association, introduced the Nakamura variety and other varieties of rice from Kyushu. The Agricultural Association was similar to that of the cooperative, Japan Agriculture (JA), in that it collectively purchases fertilizer, pesticides, and so forth, sells agricultural products, provides financing, insurance, and guidance for managing a farm. Gathering farmers who wanted to participate in the experimental crop, they began the efforts to introduce and expand the rice from Japan under the direction of the Taipei Agricultural Association using rice seedling beds, fertilizer, and expert advice. The crop was only produced once a year during the first season, but they were able to get some good results.

Initially, the project started with 69 hectares of arable land, but increased to 300 hectares. The Taipei Agricultural Association tried this not only on high ground but also in the plains having been happy with the initial results. However, the growth of the plant was insufficient. It became a widely held belief at this point that the Japanese variety of rice became acclimatized to the temperate climate over time and thus was unsuited for cultivation in Taiwan. As a result, no additional land was developed for use.

As they began to think that it was not good to seek the further introduction and expansion of the Japanese variety of rice there, the rice harvested at Lake Zhuzi, while not plentiful, looked and tasted almost exactly like the rice from Japan. What's more, it was sold among Japanese in Taiwan at a fairly high price. While there were some large risks in not having the pure strain fixed, there was value in proceeding with this variety. With this thought, they gathered, quiet adventurously, diligent farmers who were willing to try growing this variety of Japanese rice.

The Japanese variety of rice, which had been considered to be difficult to grow in Taiwan, began to show surprisingly good results likely because the island was blessed with good weather conditions. From the highlands, cultivation spread south to Taipei, Hsinchu, and Taichung with interest in it gradually increasingly among the farmers. Thanks to these diligent farmers who were prepared to take on the risk of growing this variety of rice, its cultivation expanded from Lake Zhuzi all the way to the plains of Taichung. Iso was unable to contain his happiness and surprise.

Iso describes the following episode in his report, "Hōraimai Danwa (Discourse on Hōrai Rice)." While the report uses the phrase "Hōrai Rice," in fact the variety had not yet been so named. The story concerns these diligent farmers who bravely undertook the efforts to cultivate the Japanese variety of rice that had started in the highlands around Lake Zhuzi to the plains. In it, he relates the success of a farmer from Taichung who had been encouraged by a rice dealer to try to cultivate the Japanese variety.

> The story goes that a farmer in Sharaku (present-day Shalu), in central Taiwan tried to grow the Hōrai variety in response to a solicitation from a rice trader, but the farmer's wife wouldn't agree. This led to the husband and wife fighting but the husband won the day. When the harvest time came, there was a bountiful crop, and the husband felt quite satisfied. The rice merchant came and bought up the entire account. The husband was so delighted with the money that he grabbed a wad of bills and ran indoors, calling out his beloved wife's name in a loud voice. He playfully struck his wife on the cheek with a wad of bills, saying in a very cute way, "Look at this, look at this," as if to say, "I told you so," or "See, I was right." She looked up at her husband with a smile on her face even though she was being teased.[7]

At this juncture, it was still only those diligent farmers prepared to accept the risks who were cultivating the Japanese variety of rice in the plains. However, by 1923 and 1924, the governor-general's office was unable to stop the fever in Taiwan for growing that variety.

Both Iso and Suenaga were very impressed by the cultivation undertaken by the farmers, but at the same time, they were anxious. This was because they feared that its success was simply a coincidence due to Taiwan's advantageous weather conditions, and that if the weather became bad and insects or other diseases damaged the plants, all would be lost. This concern made them extremely nervous. They knew they had to make a pure strain of the Japanese variety for the plains or else their success would be for naught. They were under a lot of pressure.

With the Japanese variety, the stalk did not grow high making it difficult for photosynthesis to occur. Moreover, there were few offshoots, which were new buds that came up near the base of the plant. Without these additional sprouts to grow into full rice plants themselves, the overall yield will be smaller. A third problem was the fact that the sprouting season varied, and as such it was difficult to identify the proper time to harvest the crop. Harvesting it would be done ineffectively.

Despite these serious problems, the cultivation fever had caught on. It was necessary therefore for them to overcome the challenges with the variety they were using. In particular, Iso and Suenaga had to develop a strain that was more stable, and they had to do so quickly. This was no ordinary task.

THE SECOND LARGEST CULTIVATION
AREA IN THE JAPANESE EMPIRE

Suenaga reviewed the basic research he had been doing from before and organized the results. To these, he added the results of the experimental planting of the Japanese variety and conducted a detailed examination.

The result was surprising, something that no one had thought of before: the number of days raising seedlings affected the development of the rice plant at the farm. In other words, until then, sixty days were used for the raising of seedlings for the Japanese variety in the first period and thirty days for the second, but Suenaga discovered that thirty days in the first period and seventeen days in the second produced surprisingly better results.

The problem with the Japanese variety had been discovered—the days truly required for cultivating of the seedlings in the nursery rice beds was shorter than what was being done at the time. The discovery of the clue to the planting of rice sprouts, which gave birth to Hōrai Rice, was made possible by Suenaga.

Suenaga was excited and went to report about it to Iso, who also confirmed the results. But neither man could figure out why the earlier planting of rice sprouts was able to produce such high results. But facts were facts.

From 1919, until the planting of rice sprouts began in 1922, Iso conducted detailed studies with the results of extensive experiments being carefully recorded to figure out the how to theorize about the planting of rice sprouts.

The correlation between the number of nursery days, the number of planting days, the plant's height, weight, subvarieties, number of days from insertion to appearance, nitrogen content of seedlings, as well as the relationship with all other basic experimental data were calculated, and the number of nursery days optimal for each variety and region were thoroughly examined. This was the most stressful time of Iso's long life with breeding rice, when the greatest amount of concentration was required.

There was something to see in the growth of production when using the method of planting rice sprouts. However, it might have been a temporary coincidence after having been stimulated by the success in production in the highlands. In order to make the method of planting rice sprouts a sure thing, it was necessary to create a pure strain based on a proper theory. Without this, it would be unlikely that production would evenly continue into the future.

Iso repeated this to himself over and over again while he continued the calculations in his laboratory at the Taichung Agricultural Experimental Station. He was eventually successful. His being able to theorize about the planting of rice sprouts was truly important.

Because of this, Iso received the "Medal of Merit with Red and White Ribbon" from the Agriculture Society of Japan (*Dainihon Nōkai*) and the Agricultural Science Prize from the Association of Japanese Agricultural Scientific Societies. Applying this theory, the methodology of rice sprout planting became the basis when drafting the "Guidelines for Cultivating" Japonica rice and submitted to the governor-general's office. The latter accepted Iso's record of accomplishments and understood the reasonability of his theoretical elucidation. It endorsed his findings and published the guidelines as its own.

With this, the governor-general's office began to support the cultivation of the Japonica rice in place of the native variety, promoting the expansion of production of carefully chosen Japonica rice. The miraculous effects of the planting of rice plants saw an immediate rise in the value of the rice crop with the cultivation of rice spreading across the country like wildfire.

On April 23, 1926, the nineteenth Annual Conference of the Greater Japan Rice Dealers Association was held at the Taihoku Railways Hotel. On the twenty-fifth, the new Japonica variety was named in a ceremony timed with the conference. Iso, who was in Singapore then, was contacted by telegram and told to return immediately to Taiwan to attend the ceremony. He did so by ship and reached the event in time.

The tenth governor-general of Taiwan, Izawa Takio, had asked Iso for suggestions about a good name for the new variety. Iso suggested "Hōrai," in addition to "Niitakamai." Izawa immediately chose "Hōrai" and made the announcement. The name, Hōrai, is a legendary land of Chinese mythology where immortals lived on mountains near the sea. Taiwan was said to have been this enchanted land. Hōrai is the name of one of the islands comprising this strong land.

However, Hōrai Rice was not completed with the creation of the rice sprout-planting method. While using this methodology (of seedling incubation), there were still improvements to be made. First, the longer the inundation period, the better before planting the seed rice of Hōrai variety. Second, because Hōrai Rice was more sensitive to fertilizer than the native variety, it was necessary to be careful when using large amounts of fertilizer. Third, because Hōrai Rice was vulnerable to insects and disease, especially a type of mold called rice blight, the planting should be done densely at a time of the year when the rice blight was unlikely to prevent it from happening. Finally, in order to dry out the unhulled rice, it should be kept in a sealed storage area.

These were some of the things that came to be understood over time. Iso and his fellow researchers in Taichung made this important information available as soon as they discovered it, and the farmers and their associations were able to make use of it working with the governor-general's office.

The brand "Nakamura" from Kyushu was the earliest seed stock brought into Taiwan that became Hōrai Rice. It was introduced toward the end of the Taishō Era (1912–1926) and the beginning of the Shōwa Era (i.e., latter 1920s). At one point in Taiwan, more than 110,000 hectares of Nakamura-originated Hōrai Rice were planted.

It was around this time, in 1926, that the Greater Japan Rice Dealers Association held their meeting. Unfortunately, the weather was bad during this first planting season and the Hōrai Rice plants became infected with mold. Approximately 40 percent of the entire cultivated area, and in some areas, 100 percent of the crops, were devastated. Iso and Suenaga were greatly disappointed by this tragedy, but they were not about to give up. They chose a variety of Japonica rice that was resistant to mold and decided to try to introduce it into Taiwan and continued their investigations.

Their efforts were rewarded when they introduced Iyo Sengoku brand of rice from Ehime Prefecture into Taiwan, replacing the Nakamura brand. They confirmed it was resistant to mold, and created a strain called "Kagiban 2 Gō" and expanded production. By 1931, "Kagiban 2 Gō" surpassed the cultivation area used for Nakamura brand. Around this time, the Taichung Agricultural Experimental Station had produced the "Taichū 65 Gō" variety using artificial breeding.

"Taichū 65 Gō" replaced "Kagiban 2 Gō" as the variety being most produced in 1932. By 1936, it became the dominant variety of Hōrai Rice, and afterward, "Hōrai Rice" became synonymous with "Taichū 65 Gō."

The origins of "Taichū 65 Gō" began with the breeding of the pistil from the brand "Kame no O," produced by a diligent farmer in the Shōnai area of Yamagata Prefecture, Abe Kameji, with the pollen of "Shinriki," an improved variety produced by a similarly diligent farmer in Hyōgo Prefecture, Maruo Jūjirō. In 1929, this variety of Japonica rice began producing results when it was introduced into Taiwan, having been improved to make "Taichū 65 Gō." That year, it was planted and there was something remarkable about the expansion of the cultivation area.

At this time, the varieties of rice taking up the largest cultivated areas in Japan were brands named "Asahi (Morning Sun)," with 330,000 hectares of cultivated land, followed by "Aikoku" with 170,000 hectares, "Shinriki" at 160,000 hectares, and "Ginbōzu" and "Bōzu" each with 140,000 hectares. Despite Taiwan not being as big as Japan, 250,000 hectares were being utilized to grow "Taichū 65 Gō." This meant that Hōrai Rice boasted the second largest area under cultivation in the Empire of Japan.

With the birth of Hōrai Rice, Iso wrote his doctoral dissertation, "Taiwan Ina no Ikushugakuteki Kenkyū (Academic Research on Breeding of Taiwanese Rice)," for which he received his PhD from the Agriculture Faculty of Hokkaido Imperial University. His work was widely praised within the governor-general's office. In order to help him develop as a leader in his field, he was rewarded for his efforts by being sent to the United States, England, and Germany for further study. Upon returning to Taiwan, he was named professor in the Agricultural Faculty of Taipei Imperial University. He was forty-four at the time. There, he continued his research and taught the next generation of agricultural experts, focusing on the theory and practice of tropical farming.

"ISO'S HUT" AT TAIPEI IMPERIAL UNIVERSITY

The first imperial university in Japan was Tokyo Imperial University, founded in 1886. Afterward came Kyoto Imperial University in 1897, Tōhoku Imperial University in 1907, Kyushu Imperial University in 1911, and Hokkaido Imperial University in 1918. These universities were followed by Keijō Imperial University in 1924 and Taipei Imperial University in 1928. Osaka Imperial University was born in 1931 and Nagoya Imperial University came in 1939.

What this means is that imperial universities were established in the Japanese colonies of Korea and Taiwan before those in Osaka and Nagoya. This is quite extraordinary. The origins of today's Seoul National University and Taiwan National University were from these imperial universities, Keijō and Taipei, respectively. There are practically no other examples of another imperial power establishing national universities in their colonies. This is a very good example of the way that Japan governed its overseas territories and is noteworthy.

Taipei Imperial University reminds me of a university in a subtropical setting, with palm trees covering the elegant architecture comprised of bricks. Then, as now, it is located on Luosifu Road (presently known as Roosevelt Rd) in the Da'an District of Taipei.

Iso's laboratory, known colloquially as "Iso's Hut," lay in a corner of this property. Built in 1925, before the establishment of the university, it was a long, simple one-story building.

The structure was built as the governor-general's office Taipei Higher Agricultural and Forestry School. However, it was absorbed into the university when Taipei Imperial University was established. Part of this became Iso Eikichi's laboratory. Next to his building was an experimental farm so wide that it did not seem to be part of the university campus. It was here that Iso worked with his colleagues on the improvement of the rice breed further. They also sought to improve the quality of various crops, such as sweet potatoes and flax, among others.

Japan was defeated in World War II and occupied by the Allies after accepting the Potsdam Declaration. Japanese troops in China, Taiwan, and French Indochina were ordered to surrender to the Chinese National Government forces. By this point, a civil war between the national government forces and the Chinese Communist Party's forces was unfolding on the Chinese continent.

磯永吉小屋
since 1925

Figure 1.2   Drawing of Iso's Hut. *Source*: (from NTU website).

At this juncture, the nationalist government took over Taiwan, creating a Taiwan Provincial Government Office in September 1945, landing two divisions (or 12,000 men) of nationalist troops and approximately 200 officials at Keelung in October. Chen Yi, who was appointed the chief executive of Taiwan Province, arrived in Taipei next. These officials used the radio to broadcast the message that Taiwan would once again become China's territory and that its inhabitants would also be under the control of the government of the Republic of China. The desires of Taiwan's residents were completely disregarded.

All of Japan's military's facilities, not to mention the buildings belonging to the governor-general's office, were confiscated, and all Japanese military personnel, dependents, and most other Japanese were forcibly repatriated to Japan. The removal of military personnel and their dependents began first. It was completed in February 1946. Next came the other Japanese living in Taiwan at the time. Many of the 200,000 Japanese who lived in Taiwan did not wish to return to Japan and requested to be able to remain in Taiwan, many who had been there for many years. The Chinese National Government did not permit this, and the repatriation was completed in April. They lost a half-century of assets and relationships. It was a tremendously sad time for them.

However, the Chinese National Government did allow for approximately 20,000 Japanese engineers, technicians, and teachers, who were considered indispensable, to remain. Professor Iso of the Taipei Imperial University was one of them. He became a technical advisor to the Agriculture and Forestry Agency of the Taiwan Provincial Government Office.

One of the reasons Iso was asked to stay on was his connection to Chen Yi, who had served as the chief executive of Fukien Province and had previously asked Iso to head a delegation in 1937 to Fukien to observe, advise, and deliver lectures in his technical field. Iso and his group spent a month there and had several opportunities to speak with Chen and to discuss rice production in the province. A decade later, when Chen was chief executive in Taiwan, he identified Iso as an important person for the future of the island and permitted him to stay. Iso did so until 1957, spending twelve years in Taiwan following the end of the war.

In 1957, Iso retired as a technical advisor to the agency and returned to Japan after having spent forty-five years in Taiwan. Upon leaving, Iso received the highest award from the Chinese National Government for contributions to Taiwan, and the Legislative Yuan voted that Iso would receive the equivalent of 1,200 kilograms of rice every year for the remainder of his life.[8] This award was said to be in line with Chen's desire to express his appreciation to Iso.

This episode shows that every person can have both a good and bad side. Chen is widely despised in Taiwan for his role in the "2.28 Incident" in which he ordered the 2,000 troops making up the 4th Division of the Military Police and 11,000 members of the Army's 21st Division who had been sent by the Chinese Nationalist Government (KMT) of Chiang Kai-shek at Chen's request to indiscriminately fire on unarmed innocent civilians. The massacre and subsequent campaign of torture and terror by those from the mainland were long covered up during the KMT dictatorship. But Chen's efforts to promote the development of rice deserve a certain amount of credit.

RETURNING HOME AFTER FORTY-FIVE YEARS

Iso was seventy-one years old when he returned to Japan from Taiwan upon retiring from the serving as the technical advisor to Agriculture and Forestry Agency of the Taiwan Provincial Government.[9] It was the first time in forty-five years for him to return to his homeland, but he had no home to return to. Born in 1886 in Fukuyama, Hiroshima Prefecture, his family home was no longer there.

Previously Iso had worked with a man, Ozawa Tarō, who was in charge of agricultural policy at the governor-general's office in Taiwan. After serving for nearly two terms as governor of Yamaguchi Prefecture from 1953 to 1960, he was elected to the House of Representatives. Another acquaintance from Taiwan was Kuwahara Masao, then serving as the vice mayor of Hōfu City in Yamaguchi Prefecture, who had been at the time the mayor of Keelung City. Kuwahara heard about Iso's return to Japan and told Ozawa of it who suggested that Iso be invited to live in Yamaguchi Prefecture and help with the prefecture's agricultural policy. Kuwahara wrote to Iso and got his acceptance and went on to design and build a home for Iso near his own in a part of Midori Town, Hōfu City.

The situation in Japan was completely different from what it had once been. Kuwahara helped Iso with getting around the city and shopping, paying close attention to the finite details and making things as easy for Iso as possible. It was the least he could do out of respect for his academic achievements and fame.

Iso had had a stroke during his time in Taiwan after the war, and while there was some paralysis in his arms and legs, he did not let that slow him down. Through Ozawa's recommendation, Iso worked as an agriculture policy specialist for prefecture, as an adjunct professor at Yamaguchi University, and as a member of the Hōfu Branch of the prefecture's Agriculture Testing Station.

When Ozawa traveled to Central and South America, he was surprised to learn that the unit crop in the north-westernmost province of Dajabón, where a lot of Japanese from Yamaguchi Prefecture settled, in the Dominican

Republic was far less than Taiwan. Upon returning to Japan, Ozawa consulted with Iso, explaining that he wanted to help. He thought that because the Dominican Republic and Taiwan were around the same latitude that Hōrai Rice would do well there. Iso explained that the Chinese National Government forbade the export of seeds, but that the seeds of the Hōrai Rice grown in Okinawa could be acquired and sent to the Dominican Republic. Ozawa went with this proposal and contacted agricultural officials in Okinawa and had the seeds sent to the Dominican Republic, thus contributing to the raising of the unit crop there.

Iso spent three years in Hōfu. He became increasingly frustrated with the lack of information on research materials there, however, and decided to move to Yokohama, closer to the capital. He bought a house in the Idogaya area. Unfortunately, his paralysis worsened, and he was forced to spend his time in recluse.

During this time, he received some good news. His research on the breeding of rice in subtropical areas won the fifty-first Japan Academy Award in 1961. There were nine recipients that year. Iso was the only agriculture specialist. The emperor and empress were in attendance, which moved Iso tremendously, causing him to cry. If his wife had been alive, she would have been there with him. He was especially sad she could not have seen him win the prize in the presence of their majesties.

Iso's health suddenly worsened after this. He went to live with his oldest daughter, Aiko, who was married to Okayama University Professor Kawaguchi Shirō and lived in the university's housing. There she took care of him. Kawaguchi stayed in Taiwan after the war as a specialist on coral reefs and had returned to Japan a little earlier than Iso, becoming a professor at the university. He and Aiko took good care of Iso in his remaining years. Iso died peacefully in January 1972, at the age of eighty-five.

He outlived his research partner, Suenaga, by more than thirty years. Suenaga had sadly died in December 1939. It would be impossible to talk about Iso's research without Suenaga's basic experiments and other contributions. Suenaga had earned the strong trust of the farmers with whom he worked in the fields of Chiayi and Taichung, and his staff at the Chiayi Agricultural Experimentation Station were overwhelmed by his diligence and intuitive power. The successful results of his idea to cultivate the seedlings in the nursery rice beds after countless experiments to prove its viability was the ultimate example of this intuitive power. Iso's research was in that sense the theoretical extension of Suenaga's practical research.

Highly interested in Hōrai Rice, the Raj of Sarawak requested Suenaga to assist in the development of the rice there. Suenaga spent two years doing so. It was the first time to see if the rice could be developed south of Taiwan in Southeast Asia. Suenaga was very excited to try it. Unfortunately, probably as a result of working so hard, he developed tuberculosis and had to return to Taiwan and was hospitalized in Taipei's best clinic. However, he could not stop thinking about improving the rice variety, and when his fever had gone down a little, he went to the Taipei Agricultural Experimentation Station's farm where he had a stroke and died on the spot. He was fifty-three.

NOTES

1. This chapter appeared in a volume entitled *Iso Eikichi Zuisōroku* ("Iso Eikichi's Random Thoughts"), a collection of essays by Iso and recollections by those close to him privately published in 1974 after his passing.

2. Gotō was also known as the civilian governor, but in this volume, director or director-general will be used to avoid confusion.

3. For Kodama's order, dated November 5, 1901, see his papers in the National Diet Library Digital Collection.

4. Bunbu Township is now part of Taipei City.

5. See Tsutsumi Kazuyuki, "1910 Nendai Taiwan no Beishu Kairyō Keikaku to Suenaga Megumu (Suenaga Megumu and the Plan to Improve Rice Varieties in Taiwan in the 1910s)," *Tōyō Shihō*, No. 12 (March 2006), p. 19.

6. *Ibid.*

7. Iso Eikichi, "Hōraimai Danwa (Discourse on Hōrai Rice)."

8. Because of Japan's restrictions on the importation of food, Iso was not allowed to receive the rice and instead was paid in cash, after the Food Agency (*Shokuryōchō*), an external organization belonging to the then Ministry of Agriculture and Forestry, that was dissolved in 2003, purchased it on his behalf and gave him the money.

9. The Taiwan Provincial Government Office's status had changed to the Taiwan Provincial Government on May 16, 1947.

Chapter 2

The "Green Revolution" Brought about by Hōrai Rice

EIGHTH VERSION OF THE IMPROVED RICE VARIETY

Iso Eikichi returned to Japan in 1957. Around that time, the Tainan Agricultural Experimentation Station in the south continued to improve on the rice variety "Taichung 65 Gō" and succeeded in creating the high-yield type "Taichū Zairai 1 Gō" variety. The "Taichū Zairai 1 Gō" was not a Japonica breed but was instead a new variety created through the mating of local Indica types. The "Taichū Zairai 1 Gō" was created by taking the local type known as "Teikyaku Usen (Dee-geo-woo-gen)" which has a short stalk and mating it with an Indica type that has a long stalk and was resistant to illness. It was the first high-yield variety to be created by mating Indica types of rice.

The efforts of Iso and Suenaga Megumu bore fruit in the case of Hōrai Rice. At the same time, they saw great success in experiments with improving the variety of local rice. Using the "Taichū Zairai 1 Gō" as its seed stock, the International Rice Research Institute artificially mated it with the newly improved version of Indonesian rice called Peta to produce the well-known and conclusive variety called IR8.

The International Rice Research Institute was established in 1960 with funding from the Philippine Government, Ford Foundation, and the Rockefeller Foundation. The world's largest institute to study rice—it was located in Los Banos, within the School of Agriculture of the University of the Philippines. It is an international institute that continuously conducts research on the development of high-yield varieties from the best types it has gathered from around the world.

IR8 is the eighth improved rice variety that the IRRI made, and hence, the name. It has been called "miracle rice" because it was a dramatically improved variety that made possible the "Green Revolution" in Asia

23

Figure 2.1   Drawing of Indigenous Indonesian Rice Plant (left) and the IR8 High-Income Variety. *Source*: (courtesy of IRRI).

after being introduced into and spreading throughout Southeast Asia and South Asia. The numerous efforts of Iso and Suenaga brought about historic achievements, making it possible for all of Asia to be freed from the dilemma of the lack of food, as well as permitting countries to not only be able to supply their own food but also to export any extra food they did have.

Asian countries are generally overpopulated. Overpopulation places a huge burden on the country, such as creating a lack of cultivable land. The overpopulation of Asian countries is a result of the abundance of fertile rice plantations, centered on the alluvial soil delta formed by a large river or rivers pouring into the sea.

Rice is literally a staple food with a good balance of a wide variety of nutrients. That is, the ability of rice to support a population is much higher than that of other food crops. Asia has a dense population because of the abundance made possible by paddy rice cultivation. The number of people that can be supported by the yield per square kilometer is 15 to 25 for "slash and burn," or shifting, cultivation and 25 to 30 for dry field, or upland, rice cultivation, but the number grows to between 600 and 700 people in paddy rice fields.[1]

Agriculture in Asia used to be centered on the production of taro, Japanese yam, beans, and so forth by shifting cultivation. Rice went through a stage of upland rice production called *okabo*, and then reached the stage of paddy rice production in the alluvial soil delta. Paddy rice spread throughout Asia over the past 200 years. In particular, in the last 100 years, the development of Thailand's Menam Chao Phraya Delta, Myanmar's Irrawaddy Delta,

Bangladesh's Ganges Brahmaputra Delta, and so forth began in earnest, and rice productivity increased.

With the introduction of paddy rice, the population of Asia exploded. And the frontier of arable land gradually disappeared due to this rapid population increase. As a matter of fact, the area of arable land in Asia has not increased at all in the last twenty years. In some countries, cultivated land has decreased due to its destruction by desertification, urbanization, and the building of roads and other infrastructure.

On the other hand, the farming population in Asia did not stop growing. Thus, the per capita arable land area in Asia has had to decrease rapidly. In overpopulated Asia, agriculture has been characterized by its small-scale nature. As the population of farmers grew, the ability to increase productivity in these small areas became more and more important. Asia, in other words, has been under severe "competition" between increasing population pressure and rice yields.

Asia today has finally acquired the ability to overcome this competition. Rice yields in Asia have risen at a remarkable rate for half a century. This is the result of the development, introduction, and dissemination of high-yielding varieties that have been attempted mainly in rice farming. This is the "Green Revolution."

The native rice in Asia is the Indica species. However, the yield of native Indica is low. If fertilizers are applied to native varieties to increase yields, the stems will grow taller, and the leaves will grow too thick, causing the plant to fall down before harvesting. Increasing fertilizer investment in native species does not lead to increased rice revenue and can actually be harmful or counterproductive. In view of this situation, the International Rice Research Institute was established, and research on the development of high-yielding species was started.

In the latter half of the 1960s, the IRRI succeeded in developing a variety with abundant grains in which the plant was short and thick, so it did not easily collapse, and the leaves were upright, enabling efficient photosynthesis. This represented the appearance of a variety with a much higher yield than the native species.

The high-yielding varieties that gave rise to the "Green Revolution" are, to be precise, improved varieties with "high fertility and high yield." This is best illustrated in the history of Japan's agricultural development. The area of arable land in Japan is small compared to the number of people. Therefore, the most important theme in Japanese agriculture has been how to create new varieties with high fertilizer sensitivity.

The abolition of feudal restraints after the Meiji Restoration led to the popularization of seed exchange meetings by farmers' organizations on a nationwide scale. Through repeated crossbreeding of seeds in various regions,

"Shinriki," "Aikoku," "Kamenoo," and other varieties were developed and spread throughout the country. These techniques were called "old farmer-pastoral techniques" because they were developed by experienced farmers. This technology changed Japan's traditional farming methods and improved the productivity of rice cultivation.

In the Taishō period, natural fertilizers such as soybean meal from Manchuria were replaced by chemical fertilizers such as ammonium sulfate. In addition to the availability of chemical fertilizers at low prices, improved varieties with even higher fertilizer sensitivity than the old farming techniques were produced through the efforts of public agricultural experiment stations. Through the efforts of the public agricultural experiment stations, improved varieties that were even more sensitive to fertilizer than the old agricultural techniques were developed, such as "Asahi," "Rikuu No. 132," "Nōrin No. 1," and "Nōrin No. 8."

Taiwan's Hōrai Rice was an epoch-making achievement in improving this Japanese domestic variety to suit the soil and weather conditions of Taiwan. In fact, in the process of spreading the results of Hōrai Rice to Asia, the "Asian Green Revolution" centered on the Indica variety developed. If it were not for this agriculture revolution, food shortages and hunger would still be prevalent in Asia.[2]

A FORGOTTEN JAPANESE, SUGIYAMA TATSUMARU

Sugiyama Tatsumaru, a forgotten Japanese, helped to spread and expand Hōrai Rice in Asia.[3] He was deeply moved by the devastating starvation in the Punjab region of India and felt afterward that his life was not worth living if he did not do his utmost to help. Sugiyama was a man driven by a tragic yet brave determination.

His grandfather was Sugiyama Shigemaru, a behind-the-scenes figure who moved the leaders of Meiji Japan as an advocate of Asia, and his father was Sugiyama Yasumichi (Yumeno Kyūsaku), who dreamed of liberating Asia and worked to secure the financial resources to realize it. Tatsumaru was, in that sense, the third generation seeking to help Punjab with its hunger problem. The story of the struggle to introduce Hōrai Rice into the Punjab State and its eventual success is another important aspect behind Asia's Green Revolution.

Tatsumaru graduated from the Imperial Japanese Army Academy and was sent to the Negros Island in the Philippines, a location where the war's outcome was looking bleak for Japan. While most of the soldiers in his unit were killed in action, he was able to escape and return home. However, although he returned to Japan, it was not easy for him to find work and earn a living.

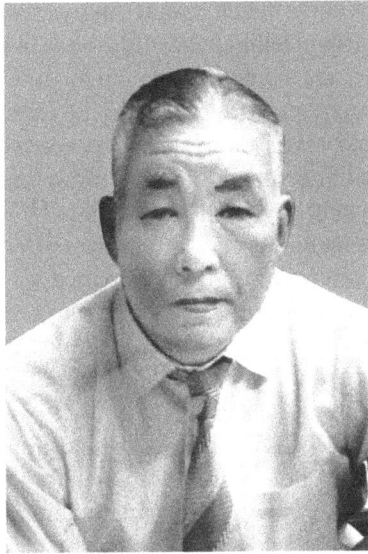

Figure 2.2   Sugiyama Tatsumaru. *Source*: (courtesy of Sankei Shimbunsha).

Finally, he built a small factory in the burned-out ruins of Akihabara, Tokyo, and was able to make ends meet by running a small business designing and assembling products using synthetic resin sheets and pipes.

His fate came to be decided by a strange chance. It happened one day in December 1955. He was returning to Tokyo Station after delivering a product ordered by someone in Kyōbashi, and as he approached the counter to buy a ticket, Sugiyama ran into Satō Yukimichi, one of his classmates at the IJAA and later at the Army Aviation Technical School in Tachikawa. It was a complete coincidence. Standing beside Satō was a handsome, young Indian man.

Despite it being quite cold, Satō was wearing a yellow Indian-style monk's robe over a white kimono and was holding a drum in his hand. Sugiyama could tell at a glance that Satō had become a priest of Nipponzan Myōhōji Temple, a religious organization affiliated with Nichirenshū. Because it was difficult to have a long conversation at the window, Sugiyama invited him to a coffee shop on the left side of the Yaesu exit. It was their first encounter since graduating from aviation school.

Sugiyama thought they were going to have a long conversation, but Satō suddenly declared that he was a member of the Nipponzan Myōhōji Temple, founded by Saint Fujii Nittatsu. He said that he believed in the philosophy of the late Master Gandhi of India and was involved in relief activities for the poor in one of the *ashrams*, a religious community in India. He added he was on his way to India soon.

Satō introduced the young Indian man to Sugiyama again. He said that he was a brilliant student from Delhi University who was involved in the expansion of the ashrams. He was supposed to go on to the United States via Japan to spread the ashram movement to Indians living there but did not have the money for the trip. Satō asked Sugiyama if he could pay for the trip. This sudden request bothered Sugiyama. He had not seen Satō in over ten years but was suddenly asked to help pay for the trip of this Indian man, whom he did not even know. Sugiyama told him he did not have that kind of money, after which he awkwardly paid for his coffee and parted ways with them.

The next day, as Sugiyama was working on a design estimate for a chemical device made of synthetic resin at his office in Akihabara, someone appeared in front of his office door, beating a drum and loudly repeating a Buddhist chant. Sugiyama went outside and saw it was Satō and the young Indian man from the day before standing behind him. He strolled into the office and said that he had come to ask for money for the young Indian man's trip to the United States. Although Sugiyama reiterated that he did not have any money, Satō refused to budge, saying that since Sugiyama had such a large office, he should have no problem paying.

A large man, Satō placed his heavy body on the floor of the office and showed no signs of moving. Annoyed with him, Sugiyama signed and sealed a promissory note and handed it to Satō. Sugiyama later ended up scrambling to pay the bill, going into debt.

THE YOUNG INDIAN MAN'S APPEAL

Fujii Nittatsu apparently had asked Satō to tell him about Sugiyama. He must have found out that his grandfather, Shigemaru, was a supporter of Rash Bihari Bose, an Indian independence activist who defected to Japan in the past, because Nittatsu later telephoned Sugiyama at his office.

The Nipponzan Myōhōji Temple was conducting relief activities at an ashram in Wardha, in the middle of the Deccan Plateau. He said that a Japanese man was working there to teach Japanese farming techniques, including nursery planting, rice planting, weeding, and harvesting. He mentioned that that person would introduce a talented Indian man to Sugiyama, and that he would like Sugiyama to meet him. Sugiyama could tell from this call that Nittatsu held deep feelings for India.

Sugiyama explained that he did not know anything about India and that he was just a technician. In an attempt to be polite, he said he might be able to help in that capacity. He did not really mean it, though, and ended the call.

Sometime later, a young man by the name of S.K. Mirmira, who had been deeply influenced by Gandhi and was involved in the ashram movement after graduating from the Department of Political Science at Delhi University, came to Sugiyama's office accompanied by the person Nittatsu had mentioned on the phone.

He seemed to be a brilliant student from a prestigious university in India, and although he appeared poor, he had a good-looking face. He said he wanted to learn the art of pottery making and return to the ashram to spread pottery production in India. The process of kneading raw materials by hand in the mud, turning the wheel, and firing the pottery in a kiln is the work of the lowest class of people in India. However, he said that he had come to Japan to learn these skills because he believed in the thinking of Master Gandhi, who said that India's development could not be expected to occur if people thought that work with one's hands was an abomination. He also said that he had studied Japanese for a year at university. Despite his faltering Japanese, Sugiyama sensed that there was something urgent and determined hidden in his words.

The next day, Mirmira came back to Sugiyama's office to show him the unglazed pottery he had made in India, along with a package of the original clay. Sugiyama saw immediately that his work was lacking. While the color was good, there was little else to praise about it.

When Sugiyama told him that he would not be able to give him the guidance he sought, Mirmira slumped his shoulders and sat down on the floor. He explained that he could not go back to India without having first learned the art of pottery making in Japan. Master Gandhi, he said, used the Indian spinning wheel *charkha* to make his own thread to visibly demonstrate the importance of making their own things to the Indian masses. India's true independence from colonialism would not be achieved, the leader argued, if India continued to rely on imports from Britain. The charkha, therefore, is a symbol of the manufacturing by the Indian people themselves, Mirmira explained, adding that he wanted to follow in the footsteps of Master Gandhi and make things by hand. Sugiyama was impacted by these words.

Sugiyama had done what he had to do after returning from the battlefield, but he realized that he had not yet done anything to truly benefit others. During the last decade, he was so busy trying to feed himself that he had no time to do anything for others. He still had not committed to helping the young man from India, but he began to think about it at this point.

THE FATE OF THREE GENERATIONS
OF THE SUGIYAMA FAMILY

Sugiyama had not been back for some time to the family farm in Kashii, Fukuoka Prefecture, which had been developed by his father, Yumeno

Kyūsaku. On his way to Fukuoka, he took Mirmira to the Imperial Shrine at Ise thinking it to be important to let him observe the history of Japanese pottery technology, starting from pottery from the Jōmon to Yayoi and Haniwa periods. Sugiyama sent a letter to his old acquaintance Hatakake Seikō, who worked at the Ise Shrine, to tell him he was bringing a young man from India to visit soon and received a positive reply.

It was spring, a time of fresh greenery. Sugiyama was extremely busy and felt that he might even collapse if he continued to work. He apologized to his customers in advance for any delay in deliveries and decided to take a week's vacation. It was the first time I had taken such a long time off since returning from military service in the Negros Islands.

Before departing, he spent a couple of days with Mirmira in a small room on the second floor of his office in Akihabara preparing for the trip. They left by train on the Tōkaidō Line headed for Ise. It was early in the morning with the sky reddish. The Tōkaidō Line runs along the Pacific coast, with the mountains looming in the distance. Sugiyama felt a sense of freedom that he had not experienced for a long time.

As the train entered Shizuoka Prefecture, southwest of Tokyo, Mt. Fuji appeared with fields of green tea bushes in the foreground. Mirmira looked on in awe. He was stunned by this sight, which he could not see in India, where there was only reddish-brown soil and sand, with the only green being weeds. They changed trains at Nagoya Station and took the Kintetsu Line to Uji Yamada Station.

It was not far to walk from the station to the Imperial Grand Shrine, also known as the Inner Shrine. As they crossed Uji Bridge, which separated the common world from the sacred, Sugiyama felt the light of the late afternoon sky shining through the thick trees and the white pebbles on the soles of his shoes. The Isuzu River was clear and beautiful, and Sugiyama felt as if his whole being was being cleansed. After washing his hands and purifying his mind before entering the grounds, Sugiyama passed through several *torii* gates and headed for the main hall of the Inner Shrine where he saw a thatched roof supported by two thick pillars made from Kiso Cyprus trees. Standing in front of the main hall of the Inner Shrine, which is set at a right angle to the ridge of the roof with about ten decorative logs covered with gold ornaments at both ends, and with two ornamental crossbeams intersecting the roof as if to pierce it.

At Sugiyama's direction, Mirmira also prayed, worshipping the way Japanese do at Shintō shrines—two reverent bows, two firm claps, followed by another bow. Mirmira was only familiar with the places that deities dwelled in India, such as huge stone or brick structures, but he seemed to have sensed the presence of a friendly consolation for human beings in this simple, yet elegant, building made of solid wood. It was not at all intimidating for him. There was no sense of transcendence. Rather, he felt that the divinity that dwelt within him might be brought out by worshipping in this main hall. Sugiyama had noticed that Mirmira had been quiet ever since the two had washed their hands in the Isuzu River.

They headed for the Jingū Chōkokan Museum, located in the middle of Mt. Kurata, halfway between the Inner and Outer Shrines. It was a stately Renaissance-style building. This is the only place in the entire Ise Grand Shrine that feels different from the rest. However, once inside, the ancient holy utensils and offerings used in the rituals of the shrine are displayed in an orderly fashion in glass. Hatakake was waiting for Sugiyama and Mirmira there, and led them on a tour of the museum, following the prescribed route.

At one point, Mirmira suddenly stopped in front of a glass-covered display cabinet made of white wood in the corner and asked Hatakake what it was. There was no one else in the museum but the three of them. In fluent English, Hatakake told him it was a bundle of rice ears grown by the Emperor him-self in a field within the Imperial Palace in Tokyo and a bundle of white silk thread made by the empress herself,

In front of this bundle of rice ears and white braid, Mirmira seems to have intuited something. Standing upright, gazing at the ears of rice and the white silk, Mirmira then knelt down on the floor and began to say some kind of prayer in what must have been Hindi. His voice gradually grew and filled the halls. After chanting, he continued kneeling on the floor for a long time and began to cry. He then started saying something that was unclear, but with a light shining in his eye. It was the first time Sugiyama had ever seen such reverent prayer.

Mirmira stood up and said that he now understood why Master Gandhi had told him that the production technology India needs was not in the West, but in Japan, and that he had to come here to learn the technology that Japan had inherited from ancient times. Sugiyama could not hide his bewilderment, but as he stared at the look of sincere understanding on Mirmira's face, his heart began to move, if only a little, to think that maybe he should try to do something useful for India through this young man first.

Following Mirmira, a number of young people from the ashram began to visit Akihabara. Through the introductions of Sugiyama and Hatakake, they learned not only pottery but also about farming tools, bamboo crafts, and so forth and returned to their ashrams in various parts of India. Sugiyama was gradually drawn to the Indian youths who were willing to dedicate their energy to helping make their countries prosperous through the ashram movement.

Sugiyama's zeal, in turn, moved the hearts of the young people he led, and it seems that his story was reported to the Indian government. In November 1962, he received a letter inviting him to attend a conference of Sarvodaya

Sammelan, a communal movement of Gandhi's disciples, to be held in a village in Maharashtra in midwestern India. Along with the name of the person in charge of the event, the invitation was sent in the joint names of three people, including Prime Minister Jawaharlal Nehru and Finance Minister Morarji Desai. The only two Japanese who received the invitation were Sugiyama and Saint Fujii Nittatsu.

Taking the opportunity of attending this conference, Sugiyama made a detailed observation of northern India from November 1962 to April of the following year. There, he witnessed the overwhelming poverty in the region and the horrific conditions of the absolute poor, who at that time were called "untouchables." Sugiyama wondered if there was anything he could do to alleviate their condition.

It was certainly a reckless decision, but it was a journey that made Sugiyama realize that what he had to do, even if it would take him the rest of his life, was to confront the poverty of India. He gradually realized that this determination was the fate that had been handed down through three generations of the Sugiyama family, and that the only way for him to come even close to the achievements of his grandfather, Shigemaru, and his father, Yasumichi, was to address the reality that he was facing for the first time in his old age. He understood that if he worked at it, he would not only be able to meet his fate head on but others would gather to help him, thereby achieving a certain amount of success. There is no escaping the fate of three generations. It is called "fate" precisely because there is no way of escaping it.

WHY OXEN STOMACHS HANG LOW
UNDER THE BLAZING SUN

The Brahmaputra River, which moves southward from the Himalayas and the Ganges River, which flows through the plains of Hindustan, join to form a vast delta. The huge amount of water produced by the confluence of the Brahmaputra and the Ganges overflows the surrounding area, meanders in all shapes and forms, and flows into the Indian Ocean as countless small and medium-sized tributaries.

If one were to travel along the Ganges, you would emerge at the plains of Hindustan. To the far right are the peaks of the Himalayas, over 7,000 meters high and covered with snow from thousands of years ago. Continuing along the Ganges River, you would come to a plain with a grayish-gray surface. There is no sign of a forest anywhere.

To the east of the plains, where the Thar Desert straddles the three states of Punjab, Rajasthan, and Gujarat, is an area where soil from the Deccan Plateau has been deposited over a long period of time. The Ganges and Indus Rivers are often thought of as great rivers with abundant water flowing freely, with water originating in the Himalayas flowing as subterranean streams deep into the plains, saturating and overflowing to the surface to form the countless rivers of the Indus.

In reality, however, there are only two seasons: the wet season and the dry season. The rainy season is from June to October, and the dry season is from October to December. In the rainy season, it rains so hard that it seems as if the bottom of the sky has fallen out, while in the dry season, the earth dries up and the sand is so high that anyone can get submerged in it.

In the rainy season, when the whirlwind blows dust into the sky, floods strike, while in the dry season, the water disappears from the surface of the earth and goes underground, and the tributaries of the Ganges dry up to the riverbed. When the temperature is over 40 ° Celsius, which is above the human body temperature, for many days, it is impossible to maintain the strength to work. In Porbandar in Gujarat, which is the birthplace of Gandhi and near the Arabian Sea, the temperature can reach 50 ° Celsius even inside. It is red-hot outside there. The intense sunlight made the plains and mountains glowing white with the heat of the fire.

Using the village of Bedchhi in Maharashtra, where the Sarvodaya Sammelan was held, as a base, Sugiyama energetically walked around the plains of Hindustan during the dry season from November 1962. Of course, he did not know at first that there was subterranean water in the plains during the dry season.

In a village in the semi-desert of Punjab, he was taking a break in the afternoon in the shade of a sparse forest when he saw a strange sight. A herd of about twenty wild oxen were gathered not under the trees, but in one spot in the sun-drenched desert, lying still on their bellies. He wondered why they were doing that in this heat. Even though he knew it was dangerous to get close to the wild beast, he was drawn to them and walked up to them within a dozen meters.

Before lying down on their stomachs, the wildebeest would scrape up the sandy surface with their feet until they reached about thirty centimeters of dark brown soil, exposing a moist area under the ground surface, where they would lie down on their stomachs.

It seemed that if they dug up about thirty centimeters into the topsoil, they felt cooler as the heat was removed when the water in the ground evaporated. Sugiyama figured that there must be a *wadi*, or dried up river, below the top-soil where the wild oxen were lying. He cut a branch of a tree with a knife to make a round stick and dug twenty to thirty centimeters into the ground. Sure enough, he found dark brown soil and felt a slight dampness on his hands.

He also tried to pull out some sparse grass, but the roots were quite deep. He pulled with all the strength he could muster, but still without success. He dug patiently on the other side with a round stick and found that the roots were more than two meters long, and Sugiyama had heard that some of the weeds were as long as three meters. The animals and plants in the area knew instinctively where the subterranean water was and were probably able to live there by relying on it. Instincts are incredible, Sugiyama thought.

Sugiyama was able to confirm during his walks around Punjab that underneath deserts and dry areas several layers of geographical formations had accumulated, and that water existed underground. Sunlight evaporates the moisture and water flow on the surface of the earth, but there was abundant underground water. Sugiyama realized if that underground water could be properly tapped to plant trees, vegetation could also be changed. He was elated by this discovery and idea. He walked from village to village in Punjab, telling his story to the village chiefs, who all gave him a suspicious look.

MEETING THE GOVERNOR OF PUNJAB

It is unclear how the governor of Punjab found out, but Sugiyama's enthusiasm reached the ears of Pattom Thanu Pillai. Sugiyama received a letter through the chief of a village during his travels, asking him to visit the governor's house in Chandigarh, the state capital. The city is located in the foothills of the Himalayas at an elevation of 321 meters above sea level.

It was the first time since he came to India that Sugiyama had entered such a large building built during the British rule in India, showing how high and strong the British colonial rulers had been in authority and power during their reign. The current occupant wanted to meet with Sugiyama. Standing in front of the gate at the governor's house, Sugiyama wondered why and if in fact it was true.

Pillai had been informed through a Gandhi ashram official that Sugiyama's grandfather, Shigemaru, had worked hard to support Rash Behari Bose. The governor seemed to have been deeply devoted to Bose. He knew that Sugiyama had been invited by Prime Minister Nehru and Finance Minister Desai to attend the Sarvodaya Sammelan convention in Maharashtra.

The steward led him down a long corridor covered with thick lampposts and invited him into the governor's office on the second floor. The governor shook Sugiyama's hand and said that he was very glad to hear that Sugiyama was interested in the development of India and wanted to know about his observations as a Japanese in Punjab as to how he could begin to improve the lives of the Indian people. He also asked why there was such a difference between Japan and India, which had developed so much, and asked Sugiyama for his honest opinions.

Although he was momentarily at a loss for words at the sudden questions, Sugiyama answered as honestly as he could. He explained that the Japanese people cherish their forests. No matter how poor they were, the Japanese never neglected to plant trees or thin out their forests to allow the trees more room to grow. However, in the plains of Hindustan, there were few forests. As such, Sugiyama argued, it was not industrialization that was the most important thing for India today. Rather, he continued, it was necessary to channel the energy of the people of Punjab into planting trees, to change the vegetation through planting, and to achieve self-sufficiency in food.

The governor agreed with him but pointed out that neither the government of Punjab nor the people had the requisite knowledge. He asked Sugiyama for his advice.

Sugiyama said the eucalyptus tree would be good. The eucalyptus is a tree that originates from southwestern Australia to Tasmania. Its greatest characteristic is that it takes less than five years from the time it is planted to the time it becomes a mature tree. No other tree grows faster than the eucalyptus. This tree grows well in dry areas. This is because the roots of the eucalyptus tree can grow up to three times as deep as the height of the ground surface.

Sugiyama explained that by sucking up the underground water, they could convert arid land into green land. If they planted eucalyptus trees in the areas where there was a lot of subterranean water from the Himalayas, he expected that in about five years, the roots of the eucalyptus trees would create an underground dam of subterranean water. If water were supplied to the area around the dam, it will be possible to increase production of rice, wheat, vegetables, and potatoes. In addition, the mature eucalyptus trees could be sold for lumber and even as pulp material, the Japanese visitor added.

Pillai listened intently to Sugiyama's struggling English and asked him how the eucalyptus trees could be obtained and where exactly they should be planted.

Sugiyama answered that the international road from Delhi to Amritsar ran almost parallel to the Himalayas for 470 kilometers and that there were probably countless subterranean streams flowing from the Himalayas along the route. He proposed planting one eucalyptus tree on each side of the road at intervals of 40 meters, creating a strip of roadside forest with a width of 20 meters, over a distance of 40 kilometers. If it were successful, he added, they could extend the distance.

The governor asked how they should finance the purchase of seedlings and pay the farmers. He was obviously concerned.

Sugiyama did not know when he would have another opportunity to meet with the governor in person and made up his mind that he had to try to assist.

He answered that he would try to help. He told the governor he would be in touch when he had more information.

Pillai stood up and strongly shook his Japanese visitor's hand. Sugiyama was committed to finding a way to help finance the project.

He decided to try to finance some of it himself by selling the family farm in Kashii, Fukuoka Prefecture, that he inherited from his father, Yasumichi. Sugiyama believed that in doing so for this purpose he was not going against the wishes of his father who had inherited the farm and expanded it from his own father, Shigemaru, a proponent of Asian nationalism who began the farm decades before.

He left the governor's house. There was not a speck of cloud in the dry season sky of Punjab; it was all blue. When he saw the blue, clear sky, he took it as a message that his father and grandfather were blessing his plans to help India by selling the family farm.

Pillai's decision was also quick. As early as the beginning of 1963, with part of the funds from the development of the Punjab road combined with proceeds from the sale of the Sugiyama farm, eucalyptus seedlings were imported from Australia, and with the cooperation of the farmers along the road, planting began. The saplings grew surprisingly fast, and when they reached a certain size, the branches were pruned and cuttings were taken, which also grew rapidly. Things proceeded according to the original plan, from 1964 to 1965.

Sugiyama's prediction was correct. The eucalyptus had taken deep root over a distance of 40 kilometers, creating subterranean dams of subterranean water that pooled in *wadis* here and there along the cold line and began to flow over the surface. Where there was an abundance of water, paddy fields grew, followed by wheat fields, and where there was little water, root vegetables, and potatoes could be harvested. Sugiyama's heart was filled with excitement as he saw the farmers' desire to increase their production. It would take some time for the plantation to reach its full length of 470 kilometers, but as long as the farmers made the effort, the reforestation movement would eventually turn into a self-sustaining one through increased food production, higher land prices, and higher income from the conversion of the land to arable areas. His prediction proved mostly correct, and his mood was unusually high.

THE FIRST TIME TO MEET A
JAPANESE PERSON LIKE YOU

Sugiyama had met Iso Eikichi in Taiwan some ten years earlier. Interested in operating a factory in Taiwan to produce fertilizers and farm equipment,

Sugiyama rented the second floor of his brother-in-law's store in Taiwan, who happened to be doing business there, and used it as a base to survey rice cultivation, soil, weather, and yield in Taipei, as well as in Taichung, Tainan, Kaohsiung, and Pingtung.

Departing Taipei, Sugiyama traveled around the entire island, and after returning to the capital, was told that for a survey such as he was doing, it was important to meet Professor Iso Eikichi. His brother-in-law offered to make the introduction.

Sugiyama of course knew of the famous Iso, but it was a mystery to him and others that Iso was still living in Taiwan after the end of the Japanese administration, having been an engineer with the governor-general's office during Japan's rule over the island. As explained in the previous chapter, Iso continued as a technical advisor to the Agriculture and Forestry Agency of the government of the Republic of China.

With a letter of introduction in hand explaining that Sugiyama was an honest man interested in selling fertilizer and farm equipment in Taiwan and had made a detailed survey of the country, Sugiyama went to the office of the technical advisor of the Agriculture and Forestry Agency and was met by the large-size Iso.

Iso told him that although Japan had occupied and administered Taiwan for more than fifty years, he was saddened that very few Japanese still took an interest in Taiwan. Furthermore, Iso said he had not met anyone like Sugiyama for the past decade. He told him that the materials Sugiyama sought were at his house and invited him over.

Iso handed him a piece of paper with his address on it, and Sugiyama visited him that evening. Iso told him he knew that Sugiyama was the grandson of the famous Shigemaru. Sugiyama was relieved that Iso raised it first, as it would have been somewhat improper for him to discuss his heritage. He felt Iso was kind to have done so, as it put him at ease.

Iso told him that the reports and other materials he needed were in his study and suggested Sugiyama come over beginning the next day to look through them and make whatever copies he wanted. Iso would inform his servants to expect Sugiyama.

He retrieved a copy of mimeographed copy of book bound by string from the study. The book was about the history of the development of Hōrai Rice, which his colleague Suenaga Megumu and he spent nearly twenty years developing. Iso said he was not sure if Sugiyama was interested in it.

Sugiyama noticed that Iso's hands were trembling faintly as he held the book. Iso explained that he had been devoting all his energy to writing the book and, in the meantime, had had a mild stroke. He told Sugiyama not to worry as he had already recovered.

Sugiyama decided to leave at this point, as it was getting late, but told Iso he planned to visit the following day to use his study. He asked Iso to give his regards to his wife and departed.

Sugiyama continued to visit Iso's home after this but at this juncture did not show a particularly strong interest in Hōrai Rice.

EUCALYPTUS FOREST ZONE

The planting of eucalyptus trees and the discharge of subterranean water into the ground in Punjab allowed the cultivation of rice and wheat to proceed relatively smoothly. In fact, photographs later taken by the U.S. National Aeronautics and Space Administration's (NASA) Landsat satellite showed that the northern side of the international road between New Delhi and Amritsar, which runs parallel to the Himalayan mountain range running east-west in the north of India, came to be covered with thick greenery and the vegetation was changing.

However, as if to coincide with this time, news of the tragedy of the massive famine that had broken out across India, causing countless people to die of starvation, reached Sugiyama, who was working at the International Culture Welfare Association in Fukuoka. The association was a charitable organization founded by him to bring together like-minded people in Japan to help India. Sugiyama decided to visit India again to see the devastation with his own eyes.

He heard that Bihar, a state in eastern India, was the worst off so he headed there first. Bihar is known as a region where starvation due to drought often occurred. Sugiyama had visited Bihar during his previous stay in India. He knew that during the period of British rule in India, from 1873 to the following year, more than 200,000 people died of starvation, including those in the surrounding states, during the famine known as the Bihar Famine.

As he traveled from the provincial capital, Patna, to Rajgir, to Buddha Gaya, to the sacred Buddhist sites where Buddha had attained enlightenment, he was struck by the harsh reality of the situation. The starvation in this once prosperous region near the Ganges was so severe that he wanted to turn his face away. Aside from a trickle of water flowing from the Ganges, the area was completely dry as far as the eye could see. The area stretched as far as the horizon in all directions, creating an endless desert-like scene.

Pillars of dust snake up from the scorching earth to the sky, and when the sun goes down, the dust turns from purple to reddish-brown in the afterglow, echoing with an eerie shade. As night falls, the wind dies down, and through the blackness, the flickering lights of the boats as they sail down the Ganges can be seen. They seemed to be lights to ward off evil spirits on the four sides of the stretcher on the boat that carried away the starving dead. If you looked closely, you could see hundreds of lights dotting the sky.

It had not rained for three years in a row in Bihar. In that situation, there was no water above the surface. All the water flowing down from the Himalayas had flowed underground, about 40 to 50 meters below the surface. No matter where you looked, there was no forest in sight. Because there were no trees, the earth's soil could not supply organic matter through the roots.

It is not just trees. Not even grass grows. As soon as grass does grow, the skinny cows and goats fight over the roots and tear them up. Dung from cows and goats is an important fertilizer. Hardened, dried dung is also used as fuel. In fact, it is the only fuel available to some people in remote areas of the world. But after three years of drought, even this natural fertilizer and fuel were no longer available.

Without forests, there is no wood charcoal. Without charcoal, it is impossible for a blacksmith to craft or refine ore into metal tools, and which means that others will not be able to possess such utensils. Not only tools but even kitchen knives are not available in the homes of the poor people in Bihar. Only after great difficulty can you find a spade of some sort in the huts of these farmers.

This sacred place of Buddhism must have had rich forests in the past. The Indus civilization was formed and developed, according to the history books, by clearing the forests along the Ganges River. Forests are also an indispensable background in Buddhist paintings of Buddha. However, there curiously was no greenery at all when Sugiyama visited. The Mahabodhi Temple in Buddha Gaya still retained its magnificent appearance with its brick structure architecture. There are countless small- and medium-sized temples scattered all over Bihar. When these temples were built, huge amounts of bricks were made by heating them, which likely caused the surrounding forests to disappear one by one as the trees were cut for fuel. Sugiyama was stunned by the absurdity of the situation, wondering how people's deep faith in religion could destroy the environment so cruelly and suicidally.

The poor are the most likely to die of starvation. Peasants suffer, but they are slightly better off, as they cultivate the land of their landlords, pay them a small fee, and then get the rest of the harvest. The most miserable are the agricultural laborers who are employed by the peasants who received only a very small wage, often in kind, to make ends meet. India has always been overpopulated. At the time Sugiyama visited, the highest population density was in Kerala, followed by Bihar. Approximately 60 percent of the population in the rural communities were agricultural laborers.

As there had been no rainfall for three years and the earth was extremely dry, agricultural laborers, who had no one to hire them, had no choice but to stay in their cave-like houses built of dirt on the blazing hot earth, trying to avoid the draining of energy. They had no other choice but simply await death. Many of the agricultural workers, perhaps as many as half of them, used to be called "untouchables" and later became known as "designated castes" or "designated tribes."

Sugiyama saw countless deaths from starvation in Bihar. The designated caste and tribe had no family register. Their records were unknown. Even though he saw the people dying of starvation himself, the Indian government incredulously reported to the United Nations that no one had died by starvation.

The reforestation zone in the state of Punjab appeared to be successful. In any case, there was no other choice but to hope for success there first, and then use it as a model to expand the results to other parts of India. Fortunately, Punjab was spared from starvation. The reforestation of eucalyptus trees between New Delhi and Amritsar did well, and the subterranean water was beginning to flow as surface water around the 3-meter-wide eucalyptus planting strip.

Sugiyama thought that if they could succeed in introducing improved rice varieties with higher yields there, they might be able to find a way to help the region. He decided he had to meet with Iso again and learn more about Hōrai Rice.

"HŌRAI RICE IS NOT JUST FOR TAIWAN"

Iso retired from his position as technical advisor to the Agriculture and Forestry Agency of the Republic of China's Taiwan Province and had returned to Japan after forty-five years of working in Taiwan. He lived for three years in Hōfu, overlooking the Suo Sea, and then moved to Idogaya in Yokohama, where he spent his retirement.[4]

Sugiyama visited Idogaya with Mohan Parikh, the son of Gandhi's first disciple, who had come to Japan and was engaged in research on agricultural machinery. Compared to the time they had met in Taiwan, Iso was clearly unhappy. Sugiyama felt it might be the last time to see him.

The starvation in India was far beyond anyone's imagination, Sugiyama told Iso. It could not be left to chance and had to be dealt with. He explained that he wanted to make Hōrai Rice take root in India, and that around the international highway in Punjab, eucalyptus trees formed a forested zone where the subterranean water moistened the ground. As water control was possible, Sugiyama wanted to transplant the technology of Hōrai Rice to India and asked for Iso's help. Mohan Parikh was silent and looked at Iso with begging eyes.

Iso went into his study and retrieved his book on the development of Hōrai Rice. Sugiyama recalled seeing the same thick bound book ten years earlier at Iso's home in Taipei.

Iso said he believed that Hōrai Rice would be useful in expanding rice production in India if ways could be devised to adapt it to Indian soil, weather, and water conditions. As he explained this, he handed the book to Parikh with trembling hands. Parikh clasped his hands together and bowed his head deeply in thanks. Sugiyama and Parikh read the book carefully that night and when they finished breathed a sigh of relief.

Subsequently, when Sugiyama was back at the office of the International Culture Welfare Association, concentrating on deciphering Iso's book, a letter arrived from Taiwan. The letter was an invitation from President Chiang Kai-shek inviting Sugiyama as one of the state guests at the 100th anniversary of the birth of Sun Yat-sen. Sugiyama's grandfather, Shigemaru, was an important person who had supported Sun Yat-sen's activities in Japan. As his descendant, Sugiyama was likely seen as an appropriate guest to invite from Japan, along with representatives of other Japanese who supported Sun Yat-sen's revolution, such as Miyazaki Tōten's orphaned son, Ryūsuke, and Yanagiwara Byakuren. The sender of the invitation was, to Sugiyama's surprise, Chiang Kai-shek himself. Sugiyama was filled with excitement at the prospect of revisiting Taiwan.

The 100th anniversary of Sun Yat-sen's birth was celebrated on November 12, 1966. The time allotted for a meeting with the president was very limited. Sugiyama had no choice but to speak briefly. He looked intently at Chiang, who reached out to shake his hand.

Sugiyama told him that having inherited the will of his grandfather, Shigemaru, he was continuing to work on behalf of Asia and had dedicated himself to helping to relieve India's poverty. The International Culture Welfare Association had been established in Fukuoka, for example, specifically for the relief of starving people in India, he explained. When Sugiyama then asked Chiang to allow him to use the Hōrai Rice developed by Dr. Iso to relieve the poverty in India, he noticed his expression change.

That night, a banquet was held for the Japanese guests. A number of high-ranking officials from the Nationalist Government were also gathered around the table. When it came time for Sugiyama to introduce himself, he explained that he was helping to alleviate poverty in India by working on a flood control project, mainly in Punjab, which was about to be a success. However, he explained, the rice yield in India was too low and the only way to salvage the situation was to introduce Hōrai Rice. He told everyone that he knew that Taiwan had broken off diplomatic relations with India (for having established relations with the People's Republic of China in April 1950) but stated that Hōrai Rice was "not Taiwan's alone" and that it was necessary to help India gain economic independence. He noted how many believers in the importance of Asian independence had sacrificed themselves to help Sun Yat-sen in the past. India, as well, had gained independence from the harsh rule of the British, but its full independence was not yet complete economically. As such, it was important that the leaders of the Republic of China help India in its quest for independence through the provision of Hōrai Rice plants.

Sugiyama spoke passionately and was in a sweat by the time he sat down. Several of the guests went over to shake his hand. He sensed that people better understood the situation.

The next day, one of the participants in the welcome dinner, asked Sugiyama to come to his office immediately. He hurried to the Control Yuan, an independent investigatory and auditing agency of the government, to meet with its president, Li Shih-tsung.

President Li told him the details needed to be worked out, but President Chiang had decided to provide twenty tons of Hōrai Rice sample to India via the Food and Agriculture Organization of the United Nations. He offered his congratulations to Sugiyama, who felt a great sense of relief.

However, he added, that since the Bandung Conference (of April 1955), India had developed closer relations with China but none with Taiwan (with whom relations had been cut off) and because the Nationalist Government decided to help India, despite this, it was necessary domestically to ban Sugiyama from coming to Taiwan for the next six years as a punishment. If the government did not do so, it would set a bad example for others, he explained. He asked that Sugiyama honor the ban.

Sugiyama did so, realizing that he was caught between international and domestic politics. Fortunately, Taiwan honored its promise and sent the Hōrai Rice to India via the FAO. The Indian government in turn sent the rice to Punjab.

Using the Gandhi ashram in Punjab as a base, Sugiyama prepared a field using water from the eucalyptus forest area along the international road between New Delhi and Amritsar, and then having made seedlings and small plants, replanted them in that field having removed any weeds. Although the farmers in the area were skeptical at first, under the strong leadership of Sushil Kumar of the Gandhi ashram, they gradually became more cooperative, moved by the enthusiasm of Sugiyama and Kumar.

The growth of the Hōrai Rice was so fast that in some places it became possible to grow the crop for three seasons. The farmers were so impressed with the results that they were eager to increase production. After three or four years of crossbreeding between rice of local Indian origin and Hōrai Rice, the rice production along the international highway in Punjab came to exceed Sugiyama's initial expectations.

In order for the Hōrai Rice to be more successful, they would have to continue to experiment with crossbreeding of the rice with those of Indian origin. Kumar accepted this advice and established an agricultural technology research institute near Amritsar to train agricultural technicians and continue the crossbreeding experiments. The results spread throughout the Punjab area and spread into the other states found in the Hindustan plains.

In recognition of Sugiyama's achievements, the Indian government decided to present him with a prototype of a stupa pagoda in Fukuoka, his hometown, modeled after the stupa style, which is the prototype of Indian stupas. It is still standing on top of Mt. Myōken on the Itoshima peninsula, which juts out into the Genkai Sea in the northwestern part of the prefecture.

However, the area is covered with thick trees and the path to the pagoda is not well-defined. Tree roots have eaten away at the base of the pagoda, its white paint peeling, and the pagoda as a whole leaning sideways.

Sugiyama was someone who made great contributions to the development of Asia in the postwar but is now becoming a "forgotten Japanese." He died of cerebral hemorrhage in Fukuoka on September 20, 1987, at the age of sixty-eight.

NOTES

1. See Kyūba Kazutake and Watanabe Tadayo, "Shizen to Nōkō (Nature and Farming)," in Yano Tōru, ed., *Tōnan Ajiagaku e no Shōtai* ("An Invitation to Southeast Asian Studies") (Tokyo: NHK Shuppankai, 1977).

2. For more on this, see Dana G. Dalyrmple, *Development and Spread of High-Yielding Wheat Varieties in Developing Countries* (Washington, DC: Agency for International Development, 1986), and Hayami Yūjirō, *Development Economics: From the Poverty to the Wealth of Nations* (Oxford: Clarendon Press, 1997).

3. This section is based on Sugiyama's writings, including *Indo o Aruite: Ganji Ō no Ato o Tsugu Hitobito* ("Walking India: The People Who Have Succeeded the Revered Gandhi") (Fukuoka: Kokusai Bunka Fukushi Kyōkai, 1966); *Kiga o Ikiru Hitobito: Ganji Ō no Undō to ha Nani ka* ("People Who Live With Starvation: What Was the Revered Gandhi's Movement About?") (Tokyo: Ushio Shuppan, 1973); and *Sabaku Ryokka ni Nozomu* ("Trying to Turn a Desert Green"), (Fukuoka: Ashi Shobō, 1984). I also referenced a book by Sugiyama's son, Mitsumaru, entitled, *Griin Fazaa: Indo no Sabaku o Midori ni Kaeta Nihonjin, Sugiyama Tatsumaru no Kiseki* ("Green Father: Sugiyama Tatsumaru, The Japanese Man Who Was Responsible for Changing a Desert into a Green Area") (Hamamatsu City, Shizuoka Prefecture: Hikumano Shuppan, 2001).

4. This phrase appears in the essay by Sugiyama in the aforementioned volume, *Iso Eikichi Zuisōroku*, published in 1974.

Chapter 3

Taiwan as a Frontier Dream

A PERFECT HIDEAWAY FOR PIRATE GROUPS

Let's take a look back at the history of Japan's rule in Taiwan.

From the southern tip of Kyushu to just above Taiwan, the island groups of Amami, Okinawa, Miyako, and Yaeyama follow one after the other. Yonaguni Island is located at the western end of the Yaeyama Group. The distance between Yonaguni Island and Taiwan Island is a little more than 100 km. You can actually see Taiwan from Yonaguni. Viewed on a map or from space, the island of Taiwan seems as if it is a part of the long, arc-shaped Japanese archipelago. After Taiwan lies the Philippines.

Taiwan faces Fujian Province on the Chinese mainland, about 150 km away. The Penghu Islands, which belong to Taiwan, lie in between, closer to Taiwan proper. Taiwan represents the easternmost island of the Eurasian continent. The Tropic of Cancer, which runs through Guangzhou, the capital of Guangdong Province in China, past the Penghu Islands, Chiayi and Mt. Yu (Yu Shan, or Jade Mountain) on Taiwan to the Pacific Ocean, runs across Taiwan.

Taiwan was first "discovered" during the Age of Discovery in the sixteenth century, when the crew of a Portuguese ship sailing in the nearby waters saw the island covered with lush greenery and praised it as a beautiful island (*a ilha formosa*). This is said to be the origin of Taiwan's name, "Formosa," in the West.

Formosa/Taiwan did not appear in world history, per se, until its discovery by the Portuguese. What little is known about the island is that it was the perfect hideaway for a group of pirates known as the "Wakō," who operated in the waters of East Asia.

Shortly thereafter, the Chinese Ming Dynasty was replaced with the Qing. The Ming rulers had not been interested in Taiwan, but Qing rulers were concerned about Taiwan out of defensive interest, fearing that it would become a stronghold for anti-Qing forces. At least until that time, there is no evidence that China considered Taiwan to be its territory or subject to its rule.

Taiwan's appearance in history did not appear until its occupation by the Dutch. A fleet of Dutch East India Company ships based in Batavia (Jakarta) on the island of Java landed near Tainan and built two fortresses, known as Zeelandja Castle (Anping Old Fort) and Provincia Castle (Chikan Tower), to serve as a base for transit trade between Europe and Asia. The Dutch also began to operate sugar plantations in the plains behind Tainan.

During this time, Spain, which had already taken possession of the Philippines, dispatched the Manila Fleet to northern Taiwan and built Fort San Domingo (Red Mao Castle) at the mouth of the Danshui (hereafter, Tamsui) River. The occupation was short-lived, hampered by resistance from the indigenous people and endemic diseases, such as malaria, and the Spanish were forced to withdraw soon after.

The rule by the Dutch continued for forty years, until it was overturned, until 1661. Zheng Chenggong (known as Koxinga) was a military vassal of the Yongli Emperor, the last emperor of the Ming Dynasty, who rebelled against the Qing Dynasty under the slogan "Oppose Qing Restore Ming." Zheng established Taiwan as the base of his anti-Qing forces and expelled the Dutch. He named his administration the Kingdom of Tungning. However, the kingdom lasted only twenty-three years due to internal conflicts and was annexed by the Qing Dynasty in the 1680s.

This is where the embryonic development of Taiwanese society began. At the end of the Dutch rule, the population of Taiwan was about 20,000. During the Zheng administration, despite the blockade of Taiwan by the Qing Dynasty, the number of immigrants from Fujian and Guangdong increased rapidly, and it is estimated that the population reached 120,000 to 150,000 by the end of this period. The blockade of Taiwan was enforced by the "Xianjie" order, which forbade residents of Fujian, Guangdong, and the other five coastal provinces to live within 30 miles of the coast, and the "sea ban," which strictly prohibited ships from entering or leaving the island. However, this ban, like most others in history, had the ironic consequence of triggering the smuggling of migrants from the coastal provinces.

Fujian and Guangdong have long been overpopulated areas. Most of the province's area is mountainous, with rivers and dispersed rice paddies making up the rest. The cultivable land area is small, and the population pressure is strong in Fujian and Guangdong.

With the establishment of the Zheng Dynasty, or the Kingdom of Tungning, it became widely known to the coastal residents that Taiwan was a region with an abundance of cultivated land in proportion to its population, and many people crossed the Taiwan Strait, known as the "Blackwater Rift," a rugged region at sea, in small boats in search of a new livelihood. The western plains of Taiwan were transformed into a society of "ethnic groups" with different languages and customs, including the Quanzhou and Zhangzhou people of Tungnan (southern Fujian) and the Hakka people of Guangdong.

In 1684, after the fall of the Zheng regime, Taiwan became the territory of the Qing Dynasty for the first time as the Fujian Province Taiwan Office.

Even so, Taiwan was considered a "foreign land" for the Qing Dynasty and as a "barbarian land" beyond the reach of the Emperor's virtue (kingship). The Qing Dynasty took possession of Taiwan for the passive purpose of preventing it from becoming a base for anti-Qing forces, but had no intention of developing or managing it. Travel to Taiwan continued to be severely restricted.

However, the desire of the Fujian and Cantonese people to migrate to the new frontier was irresistible, and Taiwan's population continued to grow during this period. At the same time, the Malayo-Polynesian people who had once made their living on the plains of Taiwan and were disparagingly called "aborigines," were forced to move to the mountainous areas of the

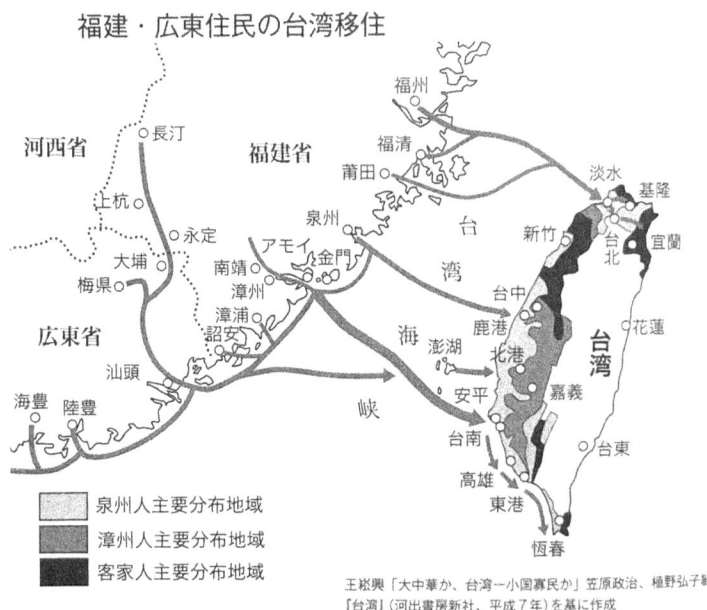

Figure 3.1   Movements of People from Mainland China to Taiwan. *Source*: (recreated from Ō Sūkō, "Daichūkaka, Taiwan, Shōkoku Kaminka," in Kasahara Masaharu and Ueno Hiroko, eds., Taiwan. p. 15)

steep Central Mountain Range that runs north-south in Taiwan as the influx of those from the mainland pushed inward.

In fact, after the Zheng Dynasty, Taiwan was almost completely uninhabited. In this era, Taiwan was a place of struggle where different ethnic groups with different origins competed for land and control. This is known as the "classification struggle." The term "classification" refers to people of different nationalities, and "struggle" refers to fighting. In the past, Taiwan was literally an "intractable island" as Han Chinese of Zhangzhou, Quanzhou, Hakka, and other ethnic groups competed with each other. Clashes between mountain tribes and Han Chinese added to the conflict.

THE OTHER SINO-JAPANESE WAR

The factors that created the beginnings of governance and provided the opportunity for social integration on this intractable island came from Japan.[1]

In October 1871, sixty-six fishermen from Miyako Island drifted ashore at Mudan in Pingtung County, southern Taiwan, where fifty-four people were killed by the native Paiwan people. At this time, Taiwan was under the jurisdiction of the Qing government. The Japanese government, therefore, sought to hold the Qing government responsible for the incident, but the Qing government sought to avoid it by claiming that Taiwan was a "foreign land." Seeing this as an opportunity, the Japanese government ordered Imperial Japanese Army Lieutenant General Saigō Jūdō to take command, and in May 1874, Saigō led a "conquering army" of 3,000 men to land and occupy the southwestern part of Taiwan. The Japanese government then negotiated with the Qing government to obtain compensation in exchange for ending the occupation.

It was the humiliation caused by Japan's invasion of Taiwan that prompted the Qing government to take a more active role in Taiwan. For the first time, the Qing government realized the risks of neglecting Taiwan. In 1885, the Taiwan Office, which had been subordinate to Fujian Province, was upgraded to the status of an independent province, Taiwan Province. Liu Ming-chuan, a Western-style bureaucrat under Li Hung-chang, was appointed the first governor. Liu worked diligently on administrative division, population and land surveys, tax collection infrastructure development, and railroad projects, collectively known as the "Qing-kuo Project."

Liu was the first to introduce the concept of development and management into a society that had been overwhelmed by inter-clan struggles and whose land, while arable, was dilapidated. However, it was not easy to make up for the long absence of administrative and social integration. A few years after assuming the post of provincial governor, Liu became ill and returned to the mainland frustrated by the lack of success. Liu's efforts to modernize Taiwan on behalf of the Qing Dynasty came into full bloom, ironically, under Japanese rule during the era of the Kodama-Gotō-led administration.

In July 1894, shortly after Liu left Taiwan, the Sino-Japanese War broke out. The Korea of the Joseon Dynasty was a tributary state of the Qing Dynasty of China. Qing had a hierarchical relationship over Joseon. China (Qing) was the "suzerain state" with Joseon the tributary country. The Qing had long taken a laissez-faire approach, but toward the end of the Joseon Dynasty, political disputes and civil wars became more frequent, and Qing troops were dispatched to the peninsula each time. Lying across the Tsushima Strait, Japan, on the other hand, came to the realization that its security could not be guaranteed unless the suzerainty relationship over Joseon by the Qing Dynasty was ended, and Joseon was allowed to exist as an independent state.

The Sino-Japanese War ended in victory for Japan. In April 1895, at the Sino-Japanese Peace Conference held at Shunpanro Hall in Shimonoseki, Japan had the Qing government recognize the full and complete independence and autonomy of Korea (Article 1) and cede the Liaodong Peninsula and Taiwan to Japan (Articles 2 & 3). Although the Liaodong Peninsula subsequently had to be returned to the Qing Dynasty due to the intervention of the so-called "Three Powers" of Russia, Germany, and France, Taiwan remained under Japanese rule for more than fifty years until Japan's defeat in World War II, when it was forced to abandon Taiwan.

Although Taiwan was claimed by Japan, the people of Taiwan did not accept it wholeheartedly. On the contrary, the people of Taiwan were so thoroughly defiant that Japan was forced to once again go to war. It was "another Sino-Japanese War," so to speak, to quell resistance.

The first governor-general of Taiwan was Imperial Japanese Navy Admiral Kabayama Sukenori. Mizuno Jun was appointed as the director of the Civil Affairs Bureau. At this point, however, the Japanese government had not prepared any laws or regulations for the administration of Taiwan. Although the Treaty of Shimonoseki settled the possession of Taiwan, there was still the difficult task of completing the procedures for the handover of Taiwan.

Kabayama negotiated with Li Ching-fang, the adopted son of Li Hung-chang and a member of the plenipotentiary committee, to cede Taiwan to Japan, on board the Qing ship "Gong Yi" and signed the related documents. Japanese forces landed at Aodi in northeastern Taiwan, from where they marched to Keelung. The Konoe Division, under Prince Kitashirakawa Yoshihisa, led the advance, fighting against Taiwanese forces who continued to resist.

The defending forces consisted of more than 50,000 soldiers from the Qing government and a local militia. The Japanese, who were better armed and outnumbered the defenders, took Keelung despite the resistance they encountered, and then proceeded to bloodlessly open Taipei, followed by occupying Tamsui.

At this point, Taipei was in an uproar. After the fall of Keelung, the defeated Qing troops poured into Taipei, where they robbed, burned, and raped the residents, and then fled to the mainland. Tang Ching-sung, the Qing government's provincial governor in Taiwan at the time, fled to Xiamen on a German steamer from Tamsui.

The northern part of the country, centering on Taipei, was conquered, and on June 17, 1895, Kabayama held a "commencement ceremony" at the Zhuanfu Gate in Taipei, where the present-day Zhongzheng Memorial Hall is located. However, only Keelung, Taipei, and Tamsui were occupied, leaving the southern areas of Taichung and Tainan unexplored. After the ceremony, the two armies fought a bloody battle for five months until Japan finally conquered Tainan.

The Qing units had already fled, leaving only ill-equipped local militia forces who used guerrilla warfare to fight the Japanese. But they had no chance. From the time Japanese troops landed in Taiwan until the fall of Tainan, the number of Japanese killed in action remained less than 3,000, while the number of Taiwanese casualties ranged from 10,000 to 15,000. The total population of Taiwan at that time was estimated to be 260,000.

In May 1888, prior to the Japanese landing at Aodi, Taiwanese elite, determined to fight the war, established the "Democratic State of Taiwan" with Provincial Governor Tang Ching-sung as president, Chiu Feng-chia as vice president, and Liu Yong-fu as general, and announced a declaration of independence forming the Republic of Formosa. However, the democratic state collapsed when Tang fled to the mainland. An attempt was made to revive the country with Liu as the new president, but it failed, and Liu also fled to the mainland.

On November 18, 1888, Kabayama declared that the entire island would be pacified. However, the intensity of anti-Japanese resistance only increased. In place of the militia, small but powerful armed groups called "local bandits" clashed with the Japanese forces in many places. The term "local bandits" meant indigenous marauders, and while there were plunderers, assaulters, and thieves, there were also chivalrous, respectable groups and proper village self-defense organizations. The types varied in character and composition, in other words. In peacetime, they hid among the townspeople and posed as "good people," but when they saw an opening in the fight against the occupying Japanese army, they went on the attack.

The first three governors-general, Kabayama, Katsura Tarō, and Nogi Maretsuke, were all army soldiers who served in the Sino-Japanese War. The period of these three governors, which began in May 1895 and lasted until February 1898, was spent fighting the local bandits.

The purpose of appointing Nogi, a particularly renowned soldier, as governor-general was literally to suppress the local bandits militarily. Nogi attempted to contain them with a tactic called "three-tier security," in which the army, civilian, or regular police, and military police each played a unique role, but he was unsuccessful. In addition to the local bandits of Han Chinese who had migrated to Taiwan, there was also a wave of anti-Japanese activity by the indigenous people living in the foothills of the Central Mountain Range, and the Japanese military found it difficult to control the rebellious groups that were popping up all over Taiwan.

Near Hsinchu, in the western foothills of the Central Mountain Range, lies Beipu, where the anti-Japanese militia was led by Tsai Ching-lin. Tsai attacked the Beipu branch of the new Japanese-led government, seizing weapons, and killing all fifty-seven Japanese living there, and was later counterattacked by the Japanese army and police, who executed him and nine other ringleaders.

Incidents of this kind engulfed the entire island. In the north, the disturbances were led by Lin Hwai-wang, Chen Qiu-ju, and Jian Da-shih; in the south-central region, Jian Yi and Ke Tie; and in the south, Zheng Ji-cheng. Without these ringleaders being caught, the rebellion would continue, and it was unlikely the Japanese administration of the island would stabilize.

In addition to the local bandits, opium smuggling had become a common practice among the residents of Taiwan. If the "opium scourge" was not eradicated, the island could not be governed properly. The morphine contained in opium is effective in calming and relieving pain caused by tropical diseases such as malaria and was even used as a household medicine in Taiwan in the past. However, the effect was only temporary, and many of them could not stop taking it after a while and became addicted. The addiction led to physical frailty, loss of vitality, weakness of the mind, and finally death. Rescuing them from the "opium scourge" was no less a challenge than suppressing the local bandits. By 1900, the number of addicts was about 170,000, or 6.1 percent of the population.

"OLD CUSTOMS" AND "LOCAL AUTONOMY"

Nogi was replaced by Kodama Gentarō who became the fourth governor-general of Taiwan. Kodama was a military man and politician who was so highly respected that it was said, "When one speaks of the Army Ministry it means 'Kodama'."[2]

War, of course, is fought by generals on the front lines. However, in order to win a large-scale foreign war, it is essential that behind the front lines, overall strategy is being planned and operations based on this strategy are

武装抗日事件分布図
1896–1932年

Figure 3.2 **Bandit Resistance against Japanese Forces, 1896–1932.** *Source*: (recreated from Taiwan Rekishi Chizu Zōteiban [Revised and Expanded Edition of Taiwan History Map], Taipei: Kokuritsu Taiwan Rekishi Hakubutsukan, undated)

being properly directed. For strategic development, it is important to have logistical support such as securing the means of troop transportation, procurement, supply, and maintenance of military equipment.

One of the merits of Kodama, the vice minister of the army, was his knowledge of logistics learned in battle during the quelling of the Satsuma Rebellion. He was also particularly knowledgeable about sanitation and the need for quarantining of countless soldiers who were returning home victorious from battle. Soldiers suffering from cholera, plague, malaria, and other diseases had to be quarantined before arriving. Kodama's quarantine project was unprecedented in scale and efficiency at the time and gained admirers in Europe and the United States.

Kodama selected Gotō Shinpei to be the frontline commander of the quarantine project and entrusted his concept to Gotō, who succeeded in the project. It was Kodama who created the opportunity for the talent of Gotō, who had served as director general of the Bureau of Health at the Ministry of Home Affairs in Tokyo and was one of the most talented bureaucrats of his generation, to truly blossom in Taiwan. It was also Kodama's good fortune to have Gotō there with him.

During this time, China was being divided up by the Great Powers. Japan had its eyes on Fujian Province across from Taiwan on the coast of the Chinese mainland, thinking that it would eventually have to come under Japan's sphere of influence. Kodama was motivated by this view.

This was the beginning of the "Kodama-Gotō administration," shortly after the beginning of the year 1898. Over the next eight years until 1906, when Kodama died suddenly after returning from the Russo-Japanese War and Gotō became the first president of the Manchuria Railway Company (South Manchuria Railway Company), that the two cooperated closely on the administration of Taiwan (serving as the advisor to successive governors-general).

To begin, they started by suppressing the local bandits and reducing the number of opium addicts. During the period of the three governors, Kabayama, Katsura, and Nogi, most of their energy had been taken up by fighting the rebellious forces and local bandits thus failing to achieve any development in Taiwan.

In fact, it was not even clear what kind of race or ethnic groups, what kind of terrain, and what kind of customs existed on this island called Taiwan. A survey of the population and land of Taiwan that was to be governed had not yet been conducted.

With the start of these land and population surveys, the suppression of the bandits and extermination of the opium scourge became urgent tasks. The crackdowns started at the same time as the surveys.

Kodama and Gotō already possessed the authority to confront difficult issues. In 1896, the No. 63 Law ("Law Concerning the Administration of Taiwan") gave the governor-general the full authority to administer Taiwan, with that area becoming its own "jurisdiction" independent of the Imperial Constitution and the Imperial Diet.

What is noteworthy is the fact that Kodama's governing policy strongly reflected the views of Gotō, who tried to realize in Taiwan the political ideas that he had cultivated during his life of hardship and isolation. It was respect for "old customs" and "local autonomy." He tried hard to instill this idea in Kodama, and fortunately it came to fruition. From the perspective of "ideology and politics," the "Kodama-Gotō administration" is a unique theme that needs to be explained further.

Taiwan, as a "foreign land," was neglected by the Qing Dynasty, and it appears to have been a disorderly society where clans were constantly fighting one another, and the opium scourge was rampant. Gotō believed that, in fact, that was not the case. In Gotō's view, "the old custom of self-government and self-defense is clearly evident" and "the custom of self-government is a kind of civil law on the island of Taiwan." In Gotō's view, the mainstay of governance was not the military, but the indigenous police force, and thus it was important for the efficient operation of the administration to return autonomy to the local levels. This was the most efficient way and was the essence of Gotō's governing beliefs.

What finally ended the local rebellion was the revival of the old Taiwanese custom of "baojia," an autonomous neighborhood organization of local community administration and policing, consisting of an average of about 100 households. Within the *baojia*, renamed the Hokō System, mutual surveillance and responsibility were thoroughly enforced, household registries created, controls on immigration put in place, epidemics prevented, roads and bridges constructed, and so forth, and an autonomous defense organization of adult-age men called the "Zhuang Ding Dan" formed. This group and the police were tasked to coordinate to eliminate places in which local bandits could freely operate.

Regarding liberating the people from the opium scourge, Gotō went about it by implementing a "Gradual Prohibition Policy." He understood that "Man cannot live without being dependent on something," and that in the modern world, where poverty and struggle were a daily occurrence, this principle was even more true. He recognized that if authorities tried to take opium away from addicts all at once, they were bound to put up a fierce resistance. It was not practical, and society would have difficulty functioning. He concluded that there was no other way but to make the opium sales business a monopoly of the governor-general, raise the monopoly price, and at the same time reduce the taxes on tobacco and alcohol to zero to change the target of addicts' dependence.

In order to maintain the monopoly, only authorized dealers were allowed to sell opium, and those who could use it were limited to those who possessed a "purchase book" (given only to those who were already addicted), and opium was gradually banned. By the beginning of the 1910s, the number of opium addicts had steadily decreased.

Thus, the "initial conditions" for the development of Taiwan were put in place. This was the start of some of Gotō's greatest work. With Kodama, a soldier-statesman of unrivaled power and authority, behind him as his protector, Gotō removed the vested interests of the arrogant military officers, scolded the bureaucrats who flinched in the face of difficult problems for their lack of enthusiasm, selected talented people from the mainland one after another, and brought their talents to full play. Gotō's tenure as director of Civil Affairs in the Taiwan governor-general's office lasted eight years. There is no other historical example of a society or a colonial nation moving toward development on such a great scale in such a short amount of time.

The establishment of the Bank of Taiwan (in 1899), land and population census projects, expansion of the tax collection base, construction of a north-south railroad, the building of ports in Keelung and Kaohsiung at the northern and southern starting/ending points of the railroad, respectively, and the development of the sugar industry were all conceived during Gotō's time, and most of them were completed before he left his post as director-general of Civil Affairs.

The vast amount of funds required for these projects were mostly dependent on government subsidies from Japan, followed by public bonds underwritten by the Bank of Taiwan. However, in 1907, the government succeeded in reducing the amount of public bonds solicited, and in 1911, it reduced the amount of central government subsidies to zero. By this time, at the very latest, the independent management of various projects had become possible.

Gotō left Taiwan in the year of Kodama's death, 1906. Each man must have left Taiwan with confidence in the success of their rule. These two men will be discussed further in chapter 6.

HEAVEN COMMANDS WHETHER IT WILL BE A GOOD HARVEST OR A BAD ONE

Returning to the story of Hōrai Rice, without the mechanism of stable water supply, it is not easy to spread and expand the revolutionary improved variety of Hōrai Rice, which was finally realized after a long and arduous process.

Hōrai Rice, as mentioned earlier, is a variety with superior characteristics compared to Taiwan's indigenous species, because it has short stalks and does not collapse before harvest. Furthermore, the uniform growth of planted rice, uniform ear emergence, high number of ears per plant and number of grains per ear, and high resistance to disease and pests makes it best.

In order for these properties to be realized, it is essential to ensure that the right amount of water flows to the field at the right time. In order to achieve this, it is necessary to prepare the arable land in a flat, even manner.

The improved varieties are new species with high fertilizer sensitivity, which means that they can produce more if they are properly fertilized. This is also true for sugarcane, the raw material for Taiwan's sugar industry, another important field. Therefore, in order for improved varieties to spread and expand, it is essential that the fertilizer applied be absorbed efficiently by the rice. In the case of natural farming, which relies solely on water from flooded rivers or natural rainwater from above, fertilizer will flow away by itself due to the force of the water, and improved varieties with high fertilizer sensitivity and high yield will not produce any results. A stable water supply mechanism is needed.[3]

Water conservancy projects, such as the construction of dams, revetments, spillways, reservoirs, and so forth, and water utilization projects to artificially control the water supply to farms, were essential. The Taiwan governor-general's office had to work on both the improvement of the rice varieties and water utilization projects at the same time.

As discussed earlier, Suenaga Megumu arrived in Taiwan to work at the Kagi (Chiayi) Farm in 1910, and Iso Eikichi was joined the Taipei Agricultural Experiment Station of the Taiwan governor-general's office in 1912. When Hatta Yoichi, who will be introduced later, is included, the fact that these three men, who would later leave their mark on the history of Taiwan's agricultural development, came to Taiwan at almost the same time is a clear indication of the governor-general's recognition that paddy rice cultivation would not be successful unless the rice variety improvement project and waterworks project were pursued together.

The summer solstice is the day with the longest time between sunrise and sunset in the northern hemisphere. In the summer solstice, the sun passes over the Tropic of Cancer. Taiwan is located on the Tropic of Cancer, entering at Chiayi and exiting at Hualien. The climate differs between the northern and southern sides of the Tropic of Cancer. The northern part of Taiwan has a subtropical climate, while the southwestern part has a tropical monsoon climate. The amount of rainfall differs greatly between the north and the southwest. In the north, the rainy season lasts from October to March of the following year. During these six months, the gentle monsoon winds blowing from the northeast of Taiwan cause the rainfall to fall quietly and evenly throughout the day, similar to the rainy season in Japan.

In contrast, the southwestern areas of Taichung, Chiayi, Tainan, and Kaohsiung enjoy dry weather during this period. However, beginning in May and continuing through September, the rainfall is intense, often accompanied by thunderstorms and windstorms. The southwestern part of the country is characterized by uneven seasonal distribution of rainfall, with extremely dry and rainy periods alternating. Furthermore, the timing and amount of rainfall fluctuates significantly from year to year, making it difficult to maintain stability during the entire process of sowing, planting, cropping, and harvesting.

Taiwan is located in the hot and humid South Seas. For this reason, it is widely assumed that two cropping seasons are possible in such an area. However, south of the Tropic of Cancer, the dry season lasts from October to March, making that impossible. It is barely possible to grow rice once a year during the rainy season from May to September. Even in the rainy season, there are years with little rainfall, making rice cultivation extremely difficult. The main rice growing areas in the southwest are Taichung, Chiayi, Tainan, and Kaohsiung. The rice fields in these areas are called "Guantian fields." A good harvest or a bad harvest depends on the providence of the heavens and in the end cannot be controlled by man. The Chianan Plain, which later became Taiwan's granary, is known as the "Chianan Dazai," were in those days the very essence of "guantian fields."

In the dry season, the southwestern part of the country is a desolate plain where the soil has dried up and hardened to the point that plowing is impossible. In the rainy season, on the other hand, farmers have to battle against overflowing rivers.

Taiwan has five central mountain ranges running north to south in the eastern part of the island, with 256 peaks over 3,000 meters above sea level. The highest peak in the Yushan Range, Mt. Yu, which was called "Mt. Niitaka" during the Japanese administration, is 3,952 meters above sea level. The Central Mountain Range is the largest spine in Taiwan. The island is divided into east and west by the steep Central Mountain Range, running north-south.

On the other hand, the rainfall flowing from the divide to the southwest will run down the steep mountains and rush across the plain, flooding the fields. The overflowing rivers often turn the Chianan Plain into a wasteland.

Once a flood occurs, the flow of water becomes so incoherent and turbulent that it is difficult to distinguish between the mainstream and its tributaries. At the northernmost point of the Chianan Plain, Taiwan's largest river, the Zhuoshui River, the distance from the foot of the mountain range to the plains is only a few kilometers, but when flooded, the river can be as wide as 40 kilometers. The river's heavy inundation carries a large amount of sediment and deposits it across the arable land. The development of the Chianan Plain involved the need to control water in the rainy season and ensure water supply in the dry season. In other words, it was about solving the problem of water and its usage.

Hatta Yoichi arrived in Taiwan in 1910, at the same time as his graduation from the Civil Engineering Department of the Tokyo Imperial University. He was assigned to work as an engineer in the Civil Engineering Division, Public Works Bureau, of the Taiwan governor-general's office. The following year, in this capacity, he undertook a survey around Taiwan, and upon his return to the governor-general's office, he was assigned to the waterworks project of Tainan City under Hamano Yashirō. In 1916, he went on another survey trip to the Philippines, Java, Borneo, Celebes, Singapore, Hong Kong, and Xiamen. After returning to Japan, he was assigned to the Audit Section of the Public Works Bureau and became the officer in charge of the construction of the hydroelectric power generation.

Immediately, in the same year, he was ordered to design and supervise the Taoyuan Irrigation Canal. The name "Pei-Shenzhen" refers to a hydraulic irrigation facility. The name "Pei" refers to the reservoir where river water is stored in a weir or dam, and "Shenzhen" refers to the waterway that draws water to the fields. In 1917, just as the construction of the Taoyuan Irrigation Canal was getting underway, Hatta was given another assignment: to conduct a survey of the Jishui River in search of a base for the construction of a power generation dam.

During the survey, Hatta was made aware of the critical importance of water supply irrigation in the southwestern Chianan Plain for the development of Taiwanese agriculture.

After making a request to the governor-general's office, he devoted his energies to a full-scale survey of irrigation in the Chianan Plain. He mobilized eighty of his subordinates to survey the area, made a detailed study of the results of the survey, and drew up a project plan for the Chianan Plain and a budget plan for the project for which he received the approval from the director of Public Works Bureau Yamagata Yōsuke, director of Civil Affairs Bureau Shimomura Hiroshi, and Governor-General Akashi Motojirō. The plan was approved by the Imperial Diet, and in 1920, construction for the Chianan Irrigation System—one of the great projects of the century—was begun.

He succeeded in supplying water to the seemingly limitless plain from the Zhuoshui River to the Zengwen River, which runs through the northernmost part of Chianan Irrigation System. Water from the Zhuoshui River and the Wushantou Dam was supplied to the fields at the end of the line in the order of trunk line, branch line, diversion line, irrigation channel, and drainage channel, with a total length of 16,000 kilometers, a distance that circles the entire island of Taiwan thirteen times. The spread and expansion of the Hōrai Rice "Kagiban No. 2" and "Taichū No. 65" also began in earnest for the first time with the hydraulic irrigation of the Chianan Plain.

TAIWAN, AN UNCHARTED FRONTIER

Hiroi Isami was one of the pioneers of modern engineering in Japan. Born in 1862, he entered Sapporo Agricultural School in the school's second year and was a classmate of Uchimura Kanzō, Nitobe Inazō, and Miyabe Kingo. The second class was taught by William Wheeler, who had replaced William Smith Clark, the first headmaster of the school. Influenced by Wheeler's personality and religious beliefs, Hiroi went to the United States by himself at his own expense two years after graduating from Sapporo Agricultural School.

With Wheeler's introduction, Hiroi received practical training as a bridge designer and railroad engineer in a design office for flood control works on the Mississippi and Missouri Rivers. After leaving the United States, he studied civil engineering and hydraulic engineering at the Universities of Karlsruhe and Stuttgart in Germany and returned to Japan to become a professor of engineering at the Sapporo Agricultural School. During this time, he helped in the construction of the ports of Akita and Hakodate. He was also involved in the construction of the Otaru Port, an unprecedented project to build a breakwater against the rough waves of the northern sea, a difficult problem that made Hiroi famous.

There is an episode that is told about Hiroi at this time. One night, when Hiroi received a report that a hoist on the breakwater under renovation was about to collapse due to fierce wind and waves, he rushed to the breakwater with his men and prevented the hoist from collapsing with all his strength. At that time, Hiroi had a pistol in his pocket. If the hoist, which was indispensable for the construction, was lost, the completion of the port would be delayed, and it would be unforgivable for the nation, which had allocated money from its meager budget for the project, and for his men, who had risked their lives for the construction. He was prepared to take his own life if the hoist collapsed out of a sense of responsibility. It did not collapse and Hiroi went on to an even brighter career.

For his achievements in the design and construction of Otaru Port, Hiroi became a professor at Tokyo Imperial University's Institute of Technology. In addition to continuing his own research, he thoroughly educated his students, including Aoyama Akira, Hatta Yoichi, and Kubota Yutaka, all highly talented men who were later known as the "Hiroi Mountains" for their amazing individual talents and the heights they achieved.

It was Hiroi's beliefs that deeply impacted the lives and thinking of his students. He used to say:

> Engineering is to shorten the distance from a few days to a few hours, to reduce the toil of a day to an hour, and in so doing to give man time to contemplate and reflect on life and to pray to God. If engineering cannot meet this challenge, then it is not worthy of being called engineering.

His saying is, on the one hand, the ultimate pragmatism and scientific spirit, and, on the other, it reveals a deep Christian faith. Hiroi was baptized, having been strongly influenced by Uchimura Kanzō, a classmate at Sapporo Agricultural School.

It was Uchimura who had made the details of the Ashio Copper Mine Poisoning Incident (that began in the late 1800s and took 100 years to address legally) known to the world. Moreover, at the time of the Russo-Japanese War, he took a non-belligerent stance along with Kōtoku Shūsui, Sakai Toshihiko, and others and advocated militant non-denominationalism. He pursued a Christian faith that was unique in Japan. He was a Christian with samurai blood, having grown up as the son of a samurai of the Takasaki Domain. However, although Hiroi was strongly inspired by Uchimura's ideas and became a Christian, he is said to have told Uchimura the following: "In this poor country, there is no use teaching religion if you can't provide food for the people. I will make my living through engineering to help the people." This religious belief in the socially vulnerable must have been the basis of Hiroi's view of the noble goal of engineering.

Hatta's conviction was strengthened by glimpses of his mentor Hiroi's beliefs during lectures and discussions, and he decided that he wanted to be like Hiroi and to cultivate himself to become such a person. Hatta became Hiroi's student and worked hard to study mountain and flood control. Upon graduation, Hiroi told Hatta, "No matter where you are on the earth, you should devote yourself to the common people and the weak of the land." It was Hiroi who urged Hatta to head to the uncharted frontier of Taiwan.

"FOR HUMANITY, FOR OUR COUNTRY"

Another person who urged Hatta to embark on frontier development overseas was Aoyama Akira, another of Hiroi's students. As soon as he graduated from the Tokyo Imperial University of Technology, Aoyama decided by himself to get involved in the construction of the Panama Canal. He journeyed alone, having received a letter of introduction from Hiroi to his friend from Columbia University, Professor William Baar. He was the only Japanese to participate in the construction of the Panama Canal.

Aoyama's struggles were truly intense. He went deep into the jungle of Panama, lived in a tent, and worked day and night in surveying. Just cutting down one of the large trees took a great deal of energy. The men working there, already tired, became susceptible to malaria and other tropical diseases, which almost always led to death.

The surveyors and engineers of the surveying group to which Aoyama belonged collapsed one after another. One day, Aoyama himself experienced severe diarrhea for reasons unknown. There was no doctor, and he recovered only after lying on his back for three or four days without eating or drinking. He must have been a man of great physical and mental strength. Aoyama was promoted, rewarded for his earnestness and devotion to work. As a professional engineer, he was engaged in the design of the dam's excess water discharge and gate opening.

However, just before the completion of the canal, he was forced to return to Japan against his will. With the intensifying anti-Japanese immigration movement in California in the United States, there were baseless rumors in Panama that Aoyama was a spy sent from Japan. As he was outnumbered, his rebuttals went unheeded, and he unhappily departed.

Nevertheless, after returning to Japan, Aoyama successfully led the Arakawa River Spillway and Shinano River Spillway projects, which were said to be among the most difficult flood control projects in Japan. These successes were all due to the knowledge and ideas he had cultivated in Panama, which he passed on to his younger colleagues. Along with Hiroi, Aoyama was the reason why Hatta was awakened to the dream of frontier development, to one day participate in an overseas project like Aoyama. The major project that Aoyama was entrusted with after returning from Panama was the Shinano River drainage canal. The monument along the river, built to commemorate the completion of the project, reads: "For Humanity, For Country." What a supple and beautiful expression!

After his assignment in Taiwan, Hatta had the opportunity to work for Hamano Yashirō, who was his senior at the Imperial College of Engineering. One of the hired "foreign experts" who had been assigned as a professor of sanitary engineering at the college was a Scottish man named William K. Burton, who was Hamano's instructor. Burton worked on development projects in Taiwan at the request of Gotō Shinpei and devoted his heart and soul to the extermination of epidemics from the unhygienic tropics and subtropics of Taiwan. Burton led the construction of water and sewage systems in Taipei, Taichung, Tainan, Keelung, Kaohsiung, and Chiayi.

At the time, Taiwan was rife with endemic diseases, such as plague, malaria, and cholera, and the average life expectancy of the islanders was around forty years old. At the start of the occupation of Taiwan, as mentioned earlier, the Japanese army fought against the insurgent forces on the island, known as "local bandits," and nearly 5,000 Japanese troops died, but of those,

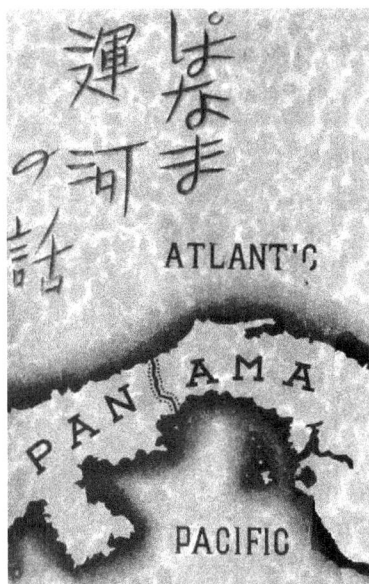

Figure 3.3   Cover of Aoyama's Notebook. *Source*: (courtesy of Sankei Shimbunsha)

only 160 died in the conflict and all the rest are said to have died of endemic diseases.

Hamano accompanied Burton to Taiwan. Three years after arriving there, Burton himself contracted malaria, and although he returned to Japan to devote himself to treatment, he died at the age of forty-three. Hamano spent the next twenty years as a "city doctor," devoting himself to transplanting his entire system of sanitary engineering to Taiwan. Hamano's belief that there are no borders when it comes to creating an environment where people can live in health and safety was also a motivating factor for Hatta to work on the Chianan Irrigation System project.

THE "SELF-INTEREST AND ALTRUISM"
OF BURTON AND HAMANO

Kanazawa in then Kaga Province, where Hatta was born and raised, is known as the Kingdom of Shinshū Buddhism, and the sect, formally known as Jōdo Shinshū, did very well here. In the Jōdo Shinshū sect, each family has a Buddhist altar enshrining Amida Buddha in the form of the Paradise of the West in the hope of being reborn in the Pure Land. On the anniversary of the death of the sect's founder, Shinran, a memorial ceremony called *hōonkō* is held, and a lecture by a priest on the teachings of Shinshū (or Shin Buddhism) is often given.

Hatta was born as the fifth son to a wealthy farming family named "Hatta-ya" in Kanazawa. In the house of his birth, there was a ten-tatami-mat Buddhist room with a large and magnificent Buddhist altar delicately decorated with gold work, about one tatami mat in size, on a dais. The Hatta family often held lectures by Shinshū priests for their relatives and neighbors, and Hatta would join them every time. The fact that Hatta spent the period of his personality development from his youth to adolescence in Kanazawa, a place with a strong religious environment, must have deeply instilled in him the concept of equality.

In Shin Buddhism, there is a phrase, "Self-interest and altruism," written with four Chinese characters. "Self-interest" is to gain merit through one's own efforts to practice Buddhism, and "altruism" is to use that merit for the salvation of others. To do both perfectly is in line with the Mahayana tradition of Buddhism. Hatta's devotional actions and beliefs he pursued during the Chianan Irrigation System project in Taiwan likely came from his upbringing in Kanazawa, which is imbued with the religious nature of Jōdo Shinshū, and the strong sense of equality there.

Hatta's philosophy of "Self-interest and Altruism" was further strength-ened by observing the actions of Hamano and his teacher, William K. Burton, who helped Hatta in Taiwan soon after he was posted there. He thought to himself watching them, "This is what self-interest and altruism are all about."

Hatta gazed at and lamented over Hamano's selflessness and infinite admiration for his teacher, Burton. For just under two years, Hatta had the opportunity to work at the construction site of the Tainan Waterworks under Hamano, a tireless engineer who had remained in Taiwan for twenty-three years and had been involved in all the sanitation and water conservancy projects in the region. This experience was a great one for Hatta. Hamano received a thorough education from Burton, a man who was the incarnation of devotion, and with Burton's spirit strongly pushing him forward, he never stopped seeking a water source in the mountains of Taiwan, where local bandits still remained and endemic diseases were rampant.[4]

When Hamano left Taiwan, he wrote down the details of his work in Taiwan in *Taiwan Suidōshi* (Taiwan Waterworks Magazine), in which he wrote the following about Burton.

The total population of the planned water supply is estimated at 1,360,000, and the maximum planned daily water supply exceeds 210,000 cubic meters. This effort is contributing to the improvement of the hygiene of the people of the island and eliminating the unfortunate illnesses of pests, typhoid, malaria, amebic dysentery, distomiasis, and others. Mr. Burton, an advisory engineer, took great pains to audit the water source of the waterworks in Taipei, and when investigating the upper reaches of the Xindian River, he wandered through the mountains and rivers to find a suitable water source, without regard for the hot and humid weather. Unfortunately, he contracted a local illness and eventually died on August 5, 1899. Ironically, he may have been the greatest casualty of the sanitary construction project. The foundation of the sanitary construction facilities on the main island, fortunately, was already established by him at that time, and through today, his plan is being continued and shared to all parts of the island.[5]

Hamano, who was deeply saddened by Burton's passing, was at the same time highly impressed by his having been involved in all the major water supply and sewage projects in Taiwan's major urban areas.

Hamano's last task was the construction of the Tainan Waterworks. The source of water for the Tainan Waterworks was the Zengwen River. Hatta was instructed by Hamano to conduct a thorough investigation of this water source. He went into the tributaries that flowed along the Zengwen River to check the water volume, water supply, and water quality, then selected the water source area and water purification area to be introduced from the Zengwen River and did his best to design water utilization facilities for water intake, water supply, water purification, and drainage.

While investigating the source of the water from the Zengwen River, Hatta became interested in the topography of the plains region that stretched from

Tainan to Chiayi, and in the course of this exploration, he wondered how the water from the Zengwen River could be supplied to the Chianan Plain. This question persisted in Hatta's mind for the rest of his life. Hamano's interest had been in building a water supply and sewage system, not necessarily in irrigating the Chianan Plain. However, if Hatta had not received Hamano's invitation to join the Tainan Waterworks Project, he might not have been able to develop the Chianan Plain later on.

THE ASTUTE DIRECTOR CHOOSES
HATTA YOICHI AS THE SUCCESSOR

Hatta was praised for his investigative skills and energy in the construction project for the Tainan Waterworks and became the most sought-after expert on water use after Hamano. Director of Civil Affairs Shimomura Hiroshi called Hatta to the governor-general's office and directed him to inspect the construction sites of water supply facilities not only in Taiwan but also in Java, Borneo, Celebes, Singapore, the Philippines, Hong Kong, Xiamen, and other surrounding areas. He would spend two months on the research trip. Hatta expressed his deep gratitude to Shimomura for providing him with a unique opportunity for comparative research and then departed.

While Shimomura judged that the prospects for the construction of the Tainan Waterworks were good thanks to the efforts of Burton, Hamano, and Hatta, the shortage of rice in the interior was becoming so acute that it was causing disturbances among the poorer-off residents, and the governor-general's office switched its attention to increasing rice production as the project to which it should devote the greatest effort.

Shimomura was invited by the sixth governor-general, Andō Sadayoshi, to become the director of Civil Affairs and served three successive governors-general, including Akashi Motojirō and Den Kenjirō who followed. Hatta's construction of Chianan Irrigation System cannot be properly discussed without mentioning the astute director of Civil Affairs Shimomura, who was an unusual administrator himself.

Upon Hatta's return from his study trip, Shimomura instructed him to formulate a plan for the construction of Taoyuan Reservoir on the plateau in the northwest part of Hsinchu Province. The Taoyuan Plateau, with its 65,000 hectares of flat land suitable for wet-rice cultivation, is located in northern Taiwan. It is surrounded by the Xue Mountain Range to the west, the Taipei Basin to the north, and the Hsinchu Plain to the south. The river flowing through the plateau was clearly lacking in water, and Hatta was given the task of finding a solution to this shortage by constructing a dam.

Due to the scarcity of water, the local people had been building reservoirs in various places for years and managed to grow rice for one crop season per year by drawing water from these reservoirs. There were about 8000 of these small reservoirs, but they were primitive and inefficient.

In 1915, Shimomura announced plans for the construction of the government-run Taoyuan Reservoir, and the Public Works Bureau of the governor-general's office made a concerted effort to conduct soil, water quantity, water quality, and triangulation surveys. Shimomura appointed Hatta as one of the leaders of the project. Hatta took the lead in drawing up the basic construction plan for Taoyuan Reservoir.

While Hatta renovated the old reservoirs and left 244 reservoirs intact, he also focused on the upper reaches of the Tamsui River that runs through the plateau. The Tamsui River flows through the north of the Taoyuan Plateau and meanders eastward. Hatta came up with the idea of building a dam called the Shihmen Water Depot. A 16-kilometer water channel was excavated starting from the Shihmen Water Depot. A number of reservoirs were constructed along the channel, and from these reservoirs, a 25-kilometer trunk canal and twelve branch canals were built, bringing the total distance of the canal system to 1,100 kilometers. This made irrigated agriculture possible on a plateau 110 meters above sea level.

The construction of the Shihmen Water Depot, the excavation of the main canal, and the building of several culverts in the middle of the water channel and branch canal were difficult projects that would later become a solid lead-in to the Chianan Irrigation System.

THE GEOSTRATEGIC IMPORTANCE OF TAIWAN

This period was the age of imperialism. Most of the Asian countries were colonies or semi-colonies of the Western powers. Under these circumstances, the geopolitical importance of Taiwan became even greater for Japan as it sought to strengthen its national power, resist the Great Powers, and expand southward. It was during the reign of the fourth governor-general, Kodama Gentarō, that the idea of using Taiwan as a base for Japan's southward expansion became even clearer. Kodama's hiring Gotō, a bureaucrat with a superior imagination and ability to implement ideas, as the civilian governor was along the lines of this larger vision to make Taiwan such a base.

Kodama said,

In order to complete the policy of Japan's southward expansion, it is necessary to encourage internal governance, strive for good neighborliness, avoid

international problems, and take measures to gain superiority in trade with the
Qing Empire and the South Seas.

This was a part of the opinion that Kodama issued as soon as he arrived at
his post as governor. This intention was passed on to the governors-general
who succeeded Kodama, Sakuma Samata, Andō Sadayoshi, Akashi Motojirō,
and Den Kenjirō. Shimomura Hiroshi would support the latter three men
as Civil Affairs director from 1915 to 1919. In Shimomura's time, Taiwan
entered an era that would prove to the world that it was the southernmost
point of the Japanese Empire.

World War I forced the powers to devote most of their energy to the
European front, and because the war was a total war of national power, the
whole of Europe, including the defeated Germany, as well as the victorious
Britain, was thoroughly affected. It was during this period that the German
philosopher Oswald Spengler's book, *The Decline of the West*, was published
and Europeans became pessimistic about the future. In contrast, Japan was
able to expand its presence in Asia.

Japan formed an alliance with Great Britain in 1902 and was able to defeat
Russia thanks to Britain's multifaceted cooperation, including the provision
of information, financial assistance, and support for the purchase of ships. In
1905, the Second Anglo-Japanese Alliance was formed, and the two countries transformed themselves into an offensive and defensive alliance, being
able to respond to attacks from third countries with mutual military support if
necessary. In 1911, with the conclusion of the third Anglo-Japanese Alliance,
the mutual obligation for stronger military cooperation between Japan and
Britain against the German threat was clearly defined. It was only natural
that Japan, a member of the Anglo-Japanese Alliance, entered World War I
on the side of Britain.

In the event that the ravages of war were to reach the British territories of
Hong Kong and Weihaiwei, the British expressed their hope that Japan would
mobilize its military forces in these areas. In response, on August 15, 1914,
the Japanese government gave an ultimatum to the German fleet to immediately withdraw from the sea area between Japan and China and to surrender
the Kiautschou Bay concession in Shandong Province to Japan on the condition that it be returned to the Qing rulers in China. With no response from
Germany, Japan declared war on Germany on the same day. In October, it
seized the Marianas, Caroline, and Marshall Islands—all German territories
in the Pacific—and in November, captured Qingdao, followed by Kiautschou
Bay and the railroad between Qingdau and Jinan.

World War I provided the perfect opportunity for Japan to emerge as a
major power. In a proposal issued in August 1914, Inoue Kaoru, a senior
statesman and former foreign and finance minister, stated, "The recent

catastrophe in Europe is a blessing in disguise for the development of Japan's national destiny in the new Taishō era."[6] In addition, Inoue argued, "The development of the new Taishō era should be based on the time of this world-wide catastrophe. The Western tendency to isolate Japan from the rest of the world should be stopped. It is Japan's time from now on."

What was this, "Western tendency to isolate Japan from the rest of the world?" It refers to the fact that the Western countries recognized Japan, which was becoming more powerful in Asia after the victory in the Russo-Japanese War, as a "yellow peril" and that this was manifested in the United States in the form of the anti-immigrant movement to ban Japanese. Inoue saw World War I as an opportunity of "providence" to "wipe out" this backward trend.

In February 1917, the decision was made to dispatch a fleet consisting of the cruiser *Akashi* and eight destroyers to the Mediterranean. Based on the island of Malta in the central Mediterranean Sea, the Japanese troops were responsible for protecting the Allied convoys, which were indispensable in the war against Germany, and made a great contribution to the reducing the tense situation in the Mediterranean in favor of the Allied forces.

Japan's entry into the war made it one of the five major powers in the world along with Britain, the United States, France, and Italy. Most importantly, the war made Japan a supply base for strategic goods to the Allies. The trade surplus generated by the war allowed Japan to repay all of its international debt, transforming itself from a debtor nation to a creditor nation. From the standpoint of economic strength, Japan was indeed in a position to become one of the five great powers.

The battles of World War I took place in Europe. As a result, the Western powers that had expanded into Asia were forced to transfer their military power from Asia back to Europe. This "vacuum" was filled by Japan. This was an opportunity for Japan to expand its presence in Asia. Taiwan was at the front line of this expansion.

NOTES

1. For this section, the author uses the following works: Itō Kiyoshi, *Taiwan: 400 Nen no Rekishi to Tenbō* (Taiwan: Four Hundred Years of History and Its Prospects) (Tokyo: Chūō Kōronsha, 1993); Ng Chiau-tong, *Taiwan Sōtokufu* (The Governor-General's Office in Taiwan), (Tokyo: Kyōikusha Rekishi Shinsho, 1981, republished in 2019 by Chikuma Shobō), and Ko Se-kai, *Nihon Tōchika no Taiwan: Teikō to Danatsu* (Taiwan Under Japanese Administration: Resistance and Oppression) (Tokyo: Tōkyō Daigaku Shuppankai, 1972).

2. For details, see Watanabe Toshio, *Gotō Shinpei no Taiwan: Jinrui mo Mata Seibutsu no Hitotsu Nari* (Gotō Shinpei's Taiwan: Improving Colonial Administration

through the Application of Biological Principles) (Tokyo: Chūō Kōron Shinsha, 2021).

3. See Hayami, *Development Economics*; Watanabe Toshio, *Kaihatsu Keizaigaku: Keizaigaku to Gendai Ajia* (Development Economics: Modern Asia and Economics) (Tokyo: Nihon Hyōronsha, 1986); and Watanabe Toshio, *Kaihatsu Keizaigaku Nyūmon* (An Introduction to Development Economics) (Tokyo: Tōyō Keizai Shinpōsha, 2010).

4. Inaba Kikuo, *Toshi no Ishi: Hamano Yashirō no Kiseki* (City Doctor: The Story of Hamano Yashirō) (Tokyo: Suidō Sangyō Shimbunsha, 1993) and Inaba Kikuo, *Baruton Sensei, Meiji Nihon o Kakeru* (Teacher Burton, Racing Around Meiji Japan) (Tokyo: Heibonsha, 2016).

5. Hamano Yashirō, "Taiwan Suidōshi (Taiwan Waterworks Magazine)," published by the Taiwan governor-general's office Public Works Bureau, 1918, available in the National Diet Library's Digital Collection.

6. Papers of Inoue Kaoru, National Diet Library.

Chapter 4

Engineers Who Did Not Give Up

THE DESOLATE CHIANAN PLAIN

The desire to modernize Taiwan grew stronger and stronger. Under the leadership of Hatta Yoichi, the construction of the Taoyuan Reservoir proceeded smoothly. One day in 1917, after finishing his work at the construction office of the Shihmen Water Depot, he was wrapping up his gaiters to go to the construction site of the water pipeline from the depot when he received a phone call. It was Yamagata Yōsuke, the head of the Civil Engineering Bureau of the governor-general's office, who was Hatta's direct superior.

Yamagata had joined the governor-general's office after graduating from the Civil Engineering Department of Tokyo Imperial College of Engineering in 1898. As director of the Civil Engineering Bureau of the governor-general's office, he drafted and supervised the construction of Kaohsiung Port and the Sun Moon Lake Hydroelectric Power Station, and above all, he was the first person to understand the importance of Hatta's project to build the Chianan Irrigation System, which was a truly amazing project at the time. Yamagata was the man who made efforts to solve the problems that sometimes hindered the way forward and who greatly helped Hatta promote the construction of the Chianan Irrigation System. Hatta was able to do what he did thanks to Shimomura and Yamagata.

Yamagata had told Hatta at one point that he had been thinking of asking him to do it for a long time but was holding off since the Taoyuan Reservoir project was under construction. He explained that Governor-General Akashi was very interested in solving Taiwan's energy problems and was particularly interested in a power generation project using the Sun Moon Lake as a water source. Yamagata told Hatta to leave the Taoyuan Reservoir project to his subordinates and asked him to investigate the water source of the Sun Moon Lake. He added that Shimomura had also recommended Hatta for the project.

Hatta was still concerned about the Taoyuan Reservoir. He knew that Yamagata had been working passionately on the Kaohsiung Port project for some time and that he had the intention of making this the largest port in Taiwan for rice and sugar by adding more quay walls and submerging the port. He also understood Yamagata's vision was in fact even greater, and he wanted to make Kaohsiung Port the base for Japan's southward expansion. Hatta would have to comply with Yamagata's request.

The amount of power generated at the time would never be enough for the construction of the Kaohsiung Port. Yamagata had often talked about the need for a large-scale power generation project to be implemented somewhere.

Yamagata's request to Hatta was to investigate the source of water for hydroelectric power generation. Yamagata said that according to his research, the Sun Moon Lake would be the best source for power generation and the Jishui River for drainage dams, but that the feasibility of such a project still needed to be explored.

Sun Moon Lake is the largest water body located in central Taiwan. The northern part of the lake is shaped like the sun and the southern part like the moon, hence the name. It is a scenic freshwater lake located at an altitude of 748 meters above sea level and has a depth of 30 meters, filled with a lot of water. The Jishui River is one of the rivers that flows through the Chianan Plain to the left of Chiayi and empties into the Taiwan Strait. Yamagata

Figure 4.1   Hatta Yoichi When He Worked at the Taiwan Governor-General's Office.
Source: (courtesy of Kanazawa Furusato Ijinkan)

wanted to investigate the effectiveness of the two, Sun Moon Lake and the Jishui River, as water sources.

It was midsummer, a time when malaria was rampant. Hatta brought quinine, which was considered to be an especially effective medicine at the time, and carried a heavy tent made of thick cotton cloth that was waterproofed. He also packed enough rice, miso, shoyu, salt, and canned goods for the journey all placed in a rucksack. He marched out with his team, but the going was rough.

Although the Sun Moon Lake did not have enough water to supply the amount Yamagata expected, Hatta informed Yamagata of the results of his survey that it might be possible if water were drawn from the largest river in Taiwan, the Zhoushui, which originates in the Central Mountain Range. After receiving Hatta's report, the governor-general submitted a detailed survey and budget for the project, and after overcoming many difficulties along the way, the project was completed in 1934.

However, Hatta decided that it would be impossible to construct a dam to divert the water in the Jishui River, which was another part of Yamagata's plan. He searched all over the tributaries of the Jishui River for a water source but could not find enough water. In addition, the steepness of the terrain made it difficult to build a dam. Yamagata accepted Hatta's decision and gave up the idea of building a dam on the Jishui River.

In the course of the field surveys, Hatta discovered a vast area of water supply, which made him wonder why he had not noticed such a suitable site before. It was when they were descending the Central Mountain Range along a tributary of the Jishui River to Chiayi. It was late in the summer and early in the autumn when the weather began to dry up. Standing on a small hill in Chiayi, he looked to the south and saw an endless expanse of desolate fields. It was the Chianan Plain.

At that time, the North-South Railroad from Keelung to Kaohsiung had already been completed. At Chiayi, Hatta took the railroad that ran the length of the island and went north into the forest where the railroad crossed the Zhoushui River. He returned to Chiayi and then headed south to Tainan, and from the window saw the wilderness of Chianan that was basically wasting away. He rode that train many times.

The Chianan area has seven rivers flowing through the plains into the Taiwan Strait from the forests in the north to Tainan in the south: the Zhuoshui, Xinhuo, Beigang, Puzi, Bazhang, Jishui, and Zengwen Rivers. During the rainy season, the riverbanks often collapse due to the amount of rainfall.

It was during the dry spell when Hatta visited, when there were only weeds and flowers growing in fierce clusters. There were no rice fields or sugarcane fields in sight. He began to think that if the water flow could be consistent and steady over the 100,000 hectares of the plains, which used to be a rain-fed rice paddy field, the suitable areas for rice and sugarcane will expand at once. Hatta became excited at the thought, his heartbeat matching the thumping of the train as it crossed the bridge over the river.

He asked his subordinates, who were accompanying him, what they thought about turning the dry plains into a large field of green, mentioning he had been thinking of it ever since arriving in Chiayi. They agreed it was a great vision but thought the project was probably too big to succeed.

Unable to give up, Hatta sent his subordinates back to the governor-general's office and remained behind alone to search for a suitable site for the dam, following his hunch that such a location existed. He got off the train at Longtian Station, walked up along the steep banks of the Zengwen River to the Guantian River, and from there hiked up to Wushantou.

The road was very steep. Hatta's legs were aching, and when he sat down to drink some water, he saw a collapsed brick structure about 50 meters ahead of him. It seemed to be part of the ruins of a brick dam built during the Dutch rule. The Dutch controlled Tainan in the early seventeenth century, having built a military fortress here, known as Zeelandja Castle, as described in the previous chapter, and Hatta had heard through legend that the walls and foundations of the fortress still existed.

In order to supply food to the people of this barren land, the Dutch must have tried some kind of irrigation system. The scale of the project was small, but there is no real difference in the way people think at any age. The Dutch rulers must have chosen Wushantou as the place to build the dam. Just as Japanese administrators would three centuries later.

The bricks were scattered all over the place, and the roots of the trees had eaten into the bricks, leaving no trace of their original shape. However, it was undoubtedly the remains of a dam.

His exhaustion suddenly disappeared, and Hatta felt some uncontrollable emotion. When he stepped into the ruins and saw the fact that there had once been an irrigation system in Wushantou, his heart began to beat wildly. This was indeed the location of the dam that he had been told had been destroyed when Zheng Cheng, a vassal of the Ming Dynasty, had challenged the Dutch by invading Tainan.

BECOMING THE AREA PROVIDING THE LARGEST AMOUNT OF RICE AND SUGAR

When Hatta returned to the governor-general's office, he borrowed dozens of maps stored in each department of the Public Works Bureau and spread them out on his work desk. He looked at all of the places along the Zhuoshui River to the Zengwen River and did calculations in his head before realizing that there was no way to bring water to the Chianan Plain other than building a dam at the upper reaches of the Guantian, a tributary of the Zengwen River, to store water.

The amount of water kept in the dam is not enough to supply the Chianan Plain. There was no other way but to draw water from the mainstream of the Zengwen River. The only way to do this would be to excavate a tunnel through Wushanling. It seems that the construction of the Wushantou Dam and the Wushanling Tunnel was necessary for the irrigation project to succeed.

Even so, the gradient of the plain was too small to supply the entire Chianan Plain with water. There are a number of trunk canals that run along the western edge of the Central Mountain Range, and from these canals there are branch canals, diversion canals, irrigation canals, and drainage canals.

Hatta wanted to confirm this, however, and undertook another survey. Hatta packed his trusty rucksack with a mess kit, rice, miso, soy sauce, tape measure, slide rule, some college notebooks, quinine and other medicines, and a trigonometer in his hand. He departed Taipei and headed south on the train, going back and forth several times between the Zhuoshui and Zengwen Rivers, between Linnei and Tainan. At Chiayi and Shinying, or sometimes Longtian, Hatta would get off and walk as far as he could on the Chianan Plain in the dry weather.

He would walk, too, on the southern areas of Shinei, wading through the branches and flowers of unnamed, short trees that battered his face. A few farmhouses stood huddled together. Hatta wondered how they made a living in such a dry region. He could hear the howling of dogs off in the distance, but it sounded rather depressing. Hatta questioned if they even had enough water to drink.

Standing on a small hillside on the way back to Chiayi Railway Station, Hatta wiped his face with a hand towel and filled his container with water. He took a sip of water and made a wish. Beyond the Alishan Mountains, the Yushan Mountains stood tall against the blue sky. He felt his tear glands relax for no reason. Standing in the midst of nature's divine beauty, people often feel as if they are being pulled into it and transformed into a transparent being. Hatta, too, felt as if he were becoming a part of nature and dissolving into it, and for a while he was in a state of sheer wonder.

Returning to the governor-general's office, he spread out the topographical map again on the worktable and started to put his own observations onto the map. He wrote small letters and formulas on each part of the map and connected the Wushantou Dam, Wushanling Tunnel, main lines, branch lines, irrigation channels, drainage channels, and so on with lines and drawings.

Hatta was sure that his ideas were gradually coming together. He decided to speak with Yamagata about it.

The Chianan Plain accounts for one-fifth of Taiwan's total arable land. It is a plain with seven rivers flowing through it, from the Zengwen River to the Zhuoshui River. It is not a small area like other plains. It is a large plain that stretches across the southern part of the North-South Railway. There is no water supply or depot there at all. It is flooded in the rainy season and dry in the dry season, and only a few paddies and sweet crops are cultivated in the favored areas. The harvest is small, and the harvest itself is extremely unstable, depending on rainfall, with damage occurring regularly from flooding.

Hatta continued with his explanation that the farmers of the Chianan Plain call the plains "rain-fed paddy fields" and said that he wanted to make a water supply facility to draw water to the plains in a stable manner. He would survey every slope of the plains and excavate a channel to distribute water equally to all areas of the plains. In doing so, the area would then become a major producer of rice and sugar. He stated that he was not unaware of the enormous amount of manpower and money that the project would require but thought that it would be well worth the effort of the entire governor-general's office. With the project completed, they would be able to turn the balance of payments around within four or five years due to the increased harvest and rising land prices.

Yamagata looked at the hand-drawn plans, knowing that there must have been a great deal of evidence for a man as calm as Hatta to speak with such an urgent tone. He told him he wanted to hear more about it and asked if he had any idea of the size of the area that could be irrigated.

As if anticipating the question, Hatta replied that his rough estimate was 100,000 hectares. He added that further surveys were necessary, but he believed that if they could directly use the water from the largest river, the Zhuoshui, the entire plain of 150,000 hectares could be covered.

Yamagata wondered if it were in fact possible to make a channel in the area, and even if that were done, where a dam could be built as the source for water.

Hatta told him he had taken a close look at the ruins of the Wushantou Dam, which were built with bricks by the Dutch during their rule over Tainan. While it was three centuries old and had completely collapsed, he said, there were still some remains of the dam. Hatta added that he had reconstructed Holland's approach in his head he came to the same conclusion that Wushantou had been the most suitable place to make the dam. If the nearby Guantian River were dammed, they would be able to secure a sufficient amount of water.

Yamagata asked if they would be able to secure enough water from the Guantian River alone, to which Hatta replied that his concept was still being developed but they would probably need to utilize the Zengwen River too. If the plan were to be adopted, it would probably require the largest budget of all the projects then underway in Taiwan. It would be even more expensive if they, he explained, were to build a tunnel to Wushanling and channel the water from the Zengwen River into the dam at Wushantou.

Yamagata was impressed at how much thought Hatta had put into the concept. He placed his hands on his head and exhaled, amazed at Hatta's bold, yet meticulous, thinking. He told him he admired him for considering so much in such a short period of time.

Yamagata stated that the real issue, then, was the budget, and that in order to move Director Shimomura, Governor-General Akashi Motojirō, and others, it was necessary to make a simple drawing and explanation so that as many people as possible could understand his concept. As he had only heard of it today, Yamagata said he had not made a decision yet and needed to be able to confidently convince the director and governor-general. He directed Hatta to come up with a plan in about a month and to undertake more detailed research to do so.

Hatta suggested that he add something about the costs of the project mentioning that he also thought it would be difficult to cover the entire cost with public funds. Although he had not been able to come up with a rough estimate yet, he knew very well that it was too large a budget for one project. He said he had an idea about how to save public money. If the project were completed, they would be able to produce products from the once-barren land, and the yield would be much higher than ordinary. Hōrai Rice could be introduced. If that were done, the price of farmland, which was practically worthless then, would rise. They could recover a part of the cost from the

Figure 4.2 Farmer Putting a Little Water in his Rain-Fed Rice Paddy. *Source*: (from Wu Ming Yun, Kanan Taishū Kensetsu Kōtei Kankai)

farmers who benefited from the project through the farmers' union, because the farmers' profits would certainly increase.

Yamagata smiled, impressed with the extent to which Hatta thought about all aspects of the project for moving forward with it, including the budget. Sensing that Yamagata, the most important person in his mind, seemed to agree with him, Hatta left the governor-general's office with some confidence. He had stood in front of Yamagata and continued to talk about his plan, never once sitting down on a chair. After leaving the governor-general's office, Hatta looked up at the autumn sky and spread his hands wide. He exhaled deeply, knowing that the project's beginning was near.

What he had told Yamagata was a very rough design. He drew on a map the huge dam at Wushantao, the Wushanling Tunnel, North and South Trunk Line, Zhuoshui Trunk Line, and so on, and calculated the scale of the expected water volume, materials equipment needed to construct the dam and tunnel, as well as an estimate of the approximate cost. He did all of this in just two weeks, a speed that surprised even himself. The work was based on photographs taken in the field, observation records, and mathematical equations written down in great detail. At this point, it was only Hatta working on it. There were still many things to be figured out. However, hoping that Yamagata would respond as soon as possible, he hurried to draw up the plan.

Assuming that the plan would be handed over to Shimomura via Yamagata, Hatta managed to come up with something close to the original plan. He was exhausted but a sense of satisfaction filled his body regarding what he had accomplished. After completing his work, he went to his favorite bar in Ximending and drank quietly but heavily, then went home and fell into a dead sleep without thinking about anything else.

After a good night's sleep, he woke up early in the morning feeling refreshed. At that time, Hatta was confident that a substantial part, if not all, of the plan would be approved by the director. After two or three days of reviewing the plan given to him by Hatta, Yamagata went to deliver it to Shimomura. After some time, they were summoned to the director's office.

AN UNSHAKEABLE FAITH IN THE PROJECT

Japan faced a severe shortage of rice after the Russo-Japanese War, and rice riots were frequent in Toyama Prefecture and other parts of Japan. Shimomura seemed to support Hatta's concept, convinced as he was that if construction proceeded as planned, the increased production of rice would greatly help to alleviate the shortage of rice there. Shimomura's deep trust in Yamagata also aided Hatta.

Shimomura was a picture-perfect bureaucrat, but he was also a poet of sorts. From a distance, Hatta was secretly fascinated by his well-rounded personality.

Shimomura said to Hatta, who stood behind Yamagata, that he had not seen him in a while but that he thought he looked well. He told Hatta that he heard Yamagata supported the concept and that if Hatta was firmly convinced of its viability, he would present it to Governor-General Akashi, along with a detailed budget, with the full force of the Public Works Bureau. He then asked if Hatta had an unshakable faith to carry this project through to completion. Hatta confirmed that he did, and from this point, this phrase, "unshakeable faith" (*Fubatsu no shinnen*), became his motto.

Akashi had become the governor-general of Taiwan in July 1918. Earlier in his military career, in anticipation of the outbreak of war between Japan and Russia, he was transferred to St. Petersburg as a senior intelligence officer of the Army General Staff. He became known for his work, after the war had begun, with providing strategic support to the dissidents of the Romanov Dynasty in Russia. In other words, Akashi contributed to the victory in the Russo-Japanese War from the rear by helping dissidents to rebel. Shimomura continued in his position as director of the Civil Affairs Bureau under Akashi when the latter became governor-general in Taiwan. How reassuring it must have been for Hatta to have had superiors like that!

Hatta learned a week after meeting Shimomura that Akashi decided to resolutely pursue the construction of the Sun Moon Lake Hydroelectric Power Station and the irrigation project for the Chianan Plain as the two major projects of the governor-general's office. This decision was conveyed to Hatta through Shimomura and Yamagata.

The details of the project were not yet finalized, but Hatta could now breathe freely knowing that they could be left to the relevant departments and subordinates. Once work started on this project, he would have to focus on it exclusively for the next few years.

After returning to Kanazawa, Hatta married Toyoki, the sixteen-year-old daughter of his doctor friend, Yonemura Kichitarō, whom his older brother, Chishō, had decided would be the perfect wife for him. For their honeymoon, they went to Nikkō for a few days and then left for Taiwan immediately after stopping off in Kanazawa.

In Taipei, the new couple took up residence in a rented house in Ximending, on the left side of the street in front of the governor-general's office on the way to the Tamsui River. It was about a twenty-minute walk to the governor-general's office. The area around the house was a chaotic place lined with Taiwanese stores. Most Japanese lived in a residential area for them, but Hatta deliberately chose this location to get to know the Taiwanese people as quickly as possible and for his young bride to have convenient access to shopping.

The day after choosing the place, Hatta went to see Director Yamagata who told him while he was away in Japan, there had been a great tailwind in support of his project. Word of his plan had spread all over the island. The provincial government sent a petition to the governor-general's office urging that the plan be realized. Indeed, the office received sixty-five letters in total with about 15,000 signatures. There were many more petitions from farmers to the provincial government as well. The willingness of the farmers to cooperate was more than had been expected, which proved to be a powerful reinforcement.

Yamagata told him in light of this, it seemed that the central government was going to subsidize the project. Supervision would of course be provided by the Civil Engineering Bureau of the governor-general's office. As for the construction, the farmers and their union would pay their share of the cost. The government had decided to provide the subsidy in installments over six years starting in 1919. Yamagata felt it was a big deal, and Hatta understood this as well.

At last, the full force of the Civil Engineering Bureau of the governor-general's office was to be devoted to the preparation of the construction plan, and Hatta was to take the lead. This was the start of the biggest project of his lifetime. It was April 1919, when Hatta was just thirty-three years old.

TAIWAN'S BIGGEST RIVER MUST BE USED

When the governor-general's office approved the establishment of the Public Wharf Association, Hatta was assigned to work as a full-time engineer at the headquarters of the association. The association's headquarters was set up in Chiayi, and Hatta moved there from Taipei with Toyoki and their daughter, Masako, who was born in April.

As soon as April arrived, the surveying, designing, and budgeting for the Chianan Irrigation System that had been initiated finally began in earnest. The surveys and research of the water supply channel, the Wushantou Dam, and the Wushanling Tunnel for the 150,000-hectare Chianan Plain were huge. In order to ensure that the project would receive government subsidies through the Imperial Diet, the data obtained from these surveys had to be meticulously recorded on the blueprints, and an official report had to be submitted to the governor-general by October, along with a detailed budget for the project. The time allotted for this preparation was six months, from April to October. Eighty young people from the Civil Engineering Bureau of the governor-general's office were assigned to work on the investigation. All of them stayed in several survey huts in Wushantou and worked tirelessly.

The survey of the Chianan Plain was endless. They had to determine the location of the three trunk lines running along the eastern edge of the plain along the Central Mountain Range, the Zhuoshui Trunk Line, the North Trunk Line, and the South Trunk Line, and plan the volume of water flowing through them. There were seven rivers in the plain, and the team needed to design a number of aqueducts to cross them. A series of waterways must be designed to supply water from the mainline to the fields through branch lines, diversion lines, and water supply channels, and finally to drain the excess water into the Taiwan Strait.

In order to distribute the water evenly, it was necessary to predict the flow rate of the waterway. To do this, it was essential to measure the slope of the plains. Carrying a triangular surveying instrument, they repeated the measurements endlessly. Fortunately, the amount of rainfall during the rainy season of 1919 was low, and they managed to complete the measurements. The survey staff slept only three or four hours a day. The results of the measurements were brought to the surveying shed, where they were included in the drawings.

It seemed at first, however, that irrigating 150,000 hectares would be impossible. Certainly, it could not be done without using Taiwan's largest river, the Zhuoshui. Irrigating 50,000 hectares was doable, and water from the Zhuoshui River could be used immediately if an intake were installed.

The Zhuoshui River originates from Mt. Hehuan in the Central Mountain Range, flows through the plain, and empties into the Taiwan Strait. It has many tributaries and is one of the largest rivers in Taiwan in terms of the watershed area. In the headwaters, black slate dust mixes with the river water, and because of the rapid flow, the dust does not settle, causing the water to appear muddy. Hence, the name of the river, whose translation means "muddy water."

If the water in the Zhuoshui River is well controlled, it can be used to irrigate the fields. In order to prevent water intake from becoming affected due to the accumulation of slate dust, effective water outlets should be constructed at the first, second, and third locations in the forest to facilitate the dredging of the accumulated sediment. The drained water that is not used for irrigation can be left in the river and discharged directly into the Taiwan Strait. The clean water released from the three water intakes would be directed into a single water trunk line, the Zhuoshui Trunk, which would be designed to gently flow into the plain.

The water released from the Zhuoshui Trunk Line as clean water (without slate dust), was to be used at first to irrigate fields in the three counties of Doulou, Huowei, and Beigang. This trunk line would provide about 50,000 hectares of water, or one-third of the water needed, for irrigating the Chianan Plain.

With this project designed, the next two large ones awaited. The biggest construction effort of the Chianan Irrigation System was that for Wushantou Dam. The other major construction project was the excavation of the Wushanling Tunnel.

The Zengwen River flows through southern Taiwan and is rich in hydraulic resources. Its headwaters are located in the Alishan Mountains, and it has various tributaries that flow downstream through the complex terrain of the mountains. The whole system is called the Zengwen River System. One of the streams in the Zengwen River System is the Guantian River. Upstream, there is a place called Wushantou, or Mt. Wushan, where small, tree-covered mountains seem to compete with each other in an intricate landscape. This is where Hatta found the ruins of the reservoir built during the Dutch reign.

Hatta thought that if a dam were built here, a considerable amount of water could be obtained not only from rainwater but also from the many streams and rivers that flow along the mountains of Wushantou. It was probably because of this topography that the Dutch once wanted to build a dam here, albeit on a small scale. If you climb a nearby mountain to view the completed Wushantou Dam, you can see the peaks of the mountains above the lake, as

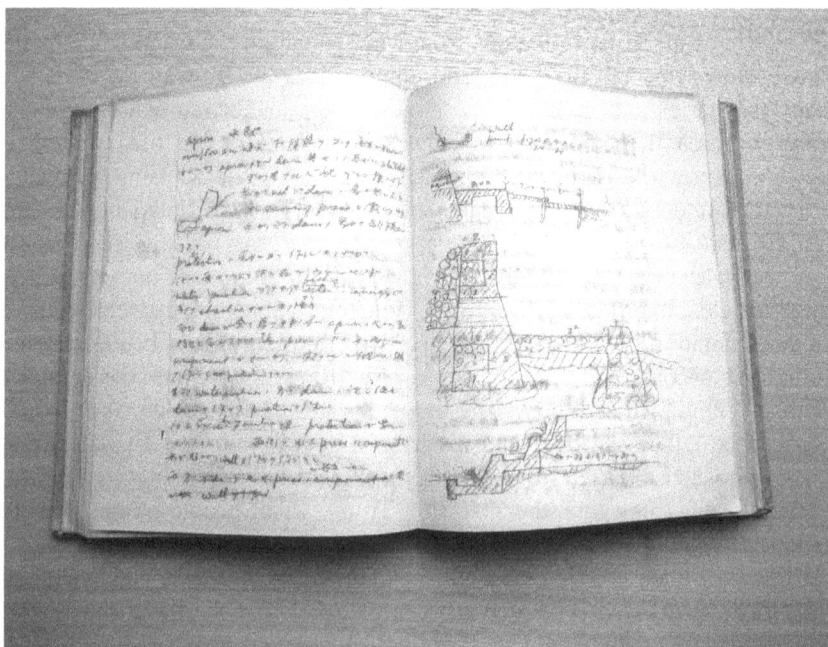

Figure 4.3 **Replica of Hatta's Notebook Entry.** *Source*: (courtesy of Kanazawa Furusato Ijinkan)

if coral was spreading its countless tentacles. This is the reason why the dam was later called the "coral lake."

Hatta believed that in order to build a dam at Wushantou and obtain enough water to irrigate the remaining 100,000 hectares, it was necessary to also use the abundant water of the Zengwen River by making a dam on it. He knew that he had to get to the top of the Wushantou Mountain Range, so he set out to explore the area around Wushantou with his staff. When they reached the top of Zhoshanling, which is located in the northern part of Wushantou, they saw the Zengwen River flowing in front of them. They pondered if they could somehow channel the water into the Wushantou Dam. Hatta wondered if it were possible to excavate a tunnel with a total length of about 3,000 meters directly underneath Wushanling and channel the water through that tunnel.

With the staff of Okura Civil Engineering Company, who would later be involved in the construction of the Wushanling Tunnel, Hatta made numerous attempts to investigate the geology. There were a few strands of petroleum running through the ground, so there was some risk. However, they came to the conclusion that there was no better place than Wushanling to channel the water from the Zengwen River to the dam. A tunnel through Wushanling was included in the plan.

Construction of the Wushantou Dam began on September 1, 1920, and that for the tunnel on June 8, 1922.

HATTA'S UNIQUE CONSTRUCTION METHOD[1]

There are concrete dams as well as rock-fill dams, which are made from rocks and gravel being piled up. It is necessary that the dam be strong enough to support the weight of the water it is meant to hold.

Everywhere, humans live on top of new strata consisting of alluvial sand and gravel that have been formed more than 10,000 years ago. However, the new stratum is too soft to build a rock-fill dam on. If you dig into the alluvial layer, you will come across the Neogene layer when you reach about 40 meters from the stratum. The Neogene layer is made up of sedimentary rocks and igneous rocks that were formed in the very distant past. A rock-fill dam could only be built on solid ground made of mountain stone.

A concrete dam was not an option for Hatta as Taiwan is located on the western edge of the Philippine Sea Plate and is an earthquake-prone area. Concrete dams are vulnerable to earthquakes. If a crack appears in a part of the concrete due to an earthquake, there is a risk that the entire dam would collapse at once from water pressure or other reasons. After repeated geological surveys, it was decided to construct the Wushantou Dam using the rock-fill dam construction method.

The size of the Wushantou Dam envisioned by Hatta was 1,273 meters long, 56 meters high, 303 meters wide at the bottom, and 9 meters wide at the top. The amount of earth, sand, rock, and other fill required to build up a dam of this size was estimated to be 540,000 cubic meters. The question was where to find such a large amount of fill, and if found, how to transport it to Wushantou.

Through a concerted search, the investigators unexpectedly found a large amount of sandstone in a group on the riverbank of Dainaisho, which is relatively close to Wushantou, only a few kilometers away. In addition, clay, silt, small sand, gravel, chestnut stones, and rocks of various sizes were all found here. When several engineers who were involved in the geological survey saw this scene on the riverbank there, they knew that they had just about all they needed and informed Hatta.

Hatta congratulated himself on his good fortune, but even though the distance was relatively short, he still had to figure out how to get the rocks and stones to Wushantou. He felt it would be inefficient to transport such a huge number of stones by hand and decided that the only way to do so was by rail.

The North-South Railroad, which had been the forerunner in the development of Taiwan, had already been fully completed between Keelung and Kaohsiung in April 1908. Because Banzida Station is located near Dainaisho, the decision was made to build a new light railroad from Dainaisho to Wushantou, and to have vehicles go back and forth frequently.

Hatta viewed the construction method as follows. Steam-powered steam shovels of various sizes were to be used to dig up the earth and stones in Dainaisho, which were then dropped into the back of "tipping earth movers" (air dump cars). The air dump cars would be transported back and forth between Dainaisho and Wushantao by steam engine. When the air dump truck arrived at Wushantao, the load of earth and stones was dropped at once below. The dam gradually grew in height. As the embankment height increased, the railroad track running over the dam was reconfigured to a higher position, and the monotonous work of piling up the earth and stones would be repeated until the entire fill reached a predetermined volume.

Two parallel dams would be constructed at intervals of 200 meters, and the two dams would eventually be connected into one. The uniqueness of Hatta's concept lies in the hydraulic fill method (water formation method). Six pumps with a diameter of 12 inches, installed near the center of the two dams, shot high-pressure water of 450 horsepower out at the tops of the ten stone groups piled up on the two embankments on either side. The force of the falling water causes the finest clay particles to flow down to the center of the weir. The clay gradually hardens in the center of the weir, forming an impermeable wall that does not allow water to flow through easily. This clay material in the center is called the core layer and is literally the core of the dam. At that

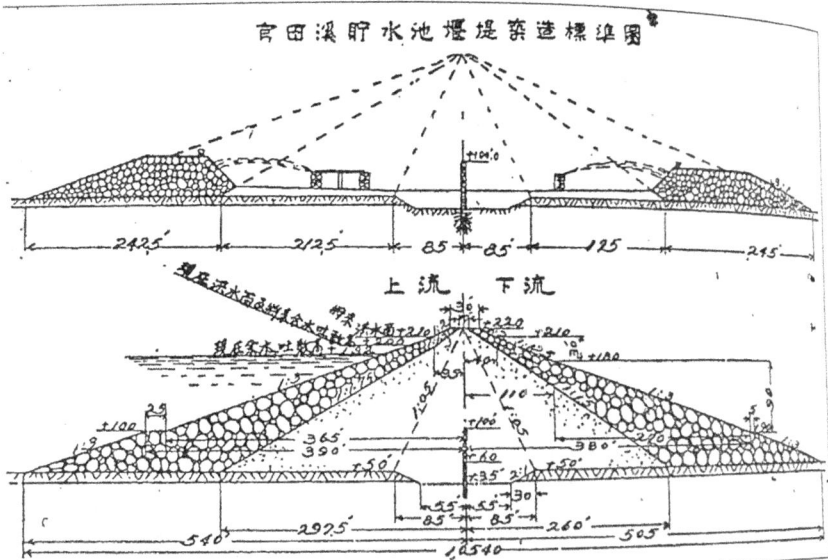

Figure 4.4 **Semi-Hydraulic Fill Method.** *Source*: (from Kōkyō Hishū Kanan Taishū Kumiai, Kōkyō Hishū Kanan Taishū Shinsetsu Jigyō Gaiyō, 1930)

time, this core layer was called the "Central Hagane Layer." It is a tough core layer, formed by clay hardened like steel, and is followed by silt, small sand, and gravel, in the order of smaller to larger particles. In addition, the entire filter layer is covered from the outside by a rock mass that does not easily fall down with the spouted water, and this structure envelops the entire dam. This is the hydraulic fill method. Hatta's concept is called the semi-hydraulic fill method, which means that it was not a completely hydraulic method. This is because the dam is not built by energy alone but also includes another process of bringing in soil, rocks, and other materials from outside.

In order to build dams efficiently, it was essential to introduce civil engineering construction equipment such as steam excavators, steam locomotives, air dump trucks, and giant pumps. Most of them were not then available for purchase in Japan. Hatta had no choice but to purchase them from the United States, the leading country in dam construction. Above all, there was the construction of the Wushanling Tunnel, for which the purchase of earth-moving equipment was also necessary.

Hatta thought that there was no other way but to go to the United States to observe the civil engineering equipment at work and operate the machines to get a feel of them. Twenty to thirty percent of the total cost of the Wushantou Dam would likely be used for the purchase of machinery from abroad. A field survey in the United States would be essential to convince the governor-general to accept the project and, more importantly, to get Public Works

Bureau Director Yamagata and the Civil Affairs Director Shimomura to agree to the project.

Just as these details were being finalized, Hatta's wife Toyoki, who was pregnant but still doing the housework, gave birth to their second daughter, Ayako. To Hatta, the birth of such a jewel-like baby, following the birth of his eldest daughter Masako and eldest son Teruo, was like a signal to go forward.

Yamagata agreed with Hatta's decision to go to the United States to learn about the machinery. After all, he thought, it was a big project, and he did not want to have any regrets about what he should have done or what he could have done better afterward. Yamagata also believed it was important for Hatta to go abroad and gain further knowledge and told him he would speak to the director about his going. He told him to prepare as best as possible to make the most of the trip. He also suggested he bring two others, Kuranari Shinichi and Shirakihara Tamitsugu, with him, as it would be a difficult trip by himself. Yamagata emphasized that the main points would be to learn about the procedures for the rock-fill method, acquire the civil engineering machines needed for the construction, and to clarify if the shield method was best for excavating the tunnel.

Kuranari, the chief of the machinery section, was excited about going to the United States. He had already started to make a list of machinery to be purchased there when he was told about Hatta's plans for the Wushantou Dam and Wushanling Tunnel. He submitted the list to Hatta, along with a rough estimate of the purchase price.

AIRBORNE ROCK DRILL

Permission for the trip to the United States was quickly granted. In March 1922, Hatta, together with Kuranari and Shirakihara, left Kaohsiung for Shanghai, where they boarded a British steamer, crossed the Pacific Ocean, landed in San Francisco, and took the transcontinental railroad to the head-quarters of the American Society of Civil Engineers in Albany, New York. It was a four-day, three-night train trip just through California, Nevada, Utah, Colorado, Kansas, Missouri, and Illinois. Gazing at the desolate wilderness, mountainous areas, and the fierce landscape that looked like the original form of the earth projected one after another on the train windows, Hatta was moved on the crossing by the pioneer spirit of the Americans, who had moved non-stop westward over the previous 200 years.

The city of Albany is the capital of New York State, overlooking the Hudson River. It is 240 kilometers north of New York City. It still retains the original landscape of continental development. Hatta felt that this city, with its diverse collection of Renaissance, Romanesque, and Art Deco architecture built by immigrants from different European countries, was very beautiful and sophisticated, and very different from Taiwan, which was still underdeveloped.

The governor-general's office had informed the American Society of Civil Engineers of the purpose of Hatta's visit in advance. Perhaps civil engineers have a sense of commonality that transcends cultures, and the leaders of the American Society of Civil Engineers welcomed the visit of Hatta and his team from Taiwan, Japan's new frontier, seeking to construct of the best dam and tunnel in the East. The American side responded to their questions with open arms. Although Hatta's English was faltering, he was able to communicate accurately because he had the technical terms imprinted in his mind.

What pleased Hatta and his team more than anything was that the governor-general's office had contacted, in advance at his request, a company that manufactured earth-moving machinery. They were also introduced to Bucyrus for steam excavators, and Siemens-Schuckert and other makers for giant pumps, and so forth. In addition, a staff member from the headquarters of the American Society of Civil Engineers accompanied them. Hatta and the others were awestruck from start to finish by the overwhelming scale and weight of the machines they saw for the first time. Hatta instructed his staff to make arrangements for the machines they wanted to purchase. His stay in the United States lasted six months.

During his travels, Hatta was newly appointed as the manager of the Wushantou Sub-branch Office, which was responsible for the front-line command and supervision of the construction of the Wushantou Dam and the Wushanling Tunnel. Upon his return to Taiwan, Hatta and his family moved to Chiayi. However, their stay there was short-lived. When the Wushantou Sub-branch Office was established, he moved to Wushantou with his family as its director.

The first major task Hatta had to tackle was the excavation of the Wushanling Tunnel. It was designed to divert or transport 50 tons of water per second from the Zengwen River channel through a winding, underground drain into a 3,109m tunnel from which it will pass once again another drain and channel into the dam.

Based on Hatta's concept for the design, a tender was held for a construction contractor. The aforementioned Okura Civil Engineering, which had a good track record for its projects with the North-South Railway and the Taoyuan Reservoir, won the bid for the Wushanling Tunnel and the main part of the Wushantou Dam. The person in charge of the bidding from Okura Civil Engineering was Fujie Junzaburō.

On the day of the bidding, Fujie met Hatta for the first time and learned that Hatta was very nervous about the tunnel excavation. At the same time, the largest tunnel construction project in Japan was the Tanna Tunnel, which ran from Atami to the entrance of Mishima in Kanagawa Prefecture on the Tōkaidō Line. The construction of the Tanna Tunnel began in March 1918, but it took sixteen years to complete instead of the expected seven years and was a difficult project that resulted in sixty-seven deaths. The Tanna Tunnel, touted as the best in the East at the time, had an inner diameter of 8.4 meters. The Wushanling Tunnel was to exceed that, having an inner diameter of 9 meters.

Hatta's idea was that the shield-tunneling method was the only way to obtain the estimated amount of water supply as quickly as possible. The shield-tunneling method involves the use of a cylindrical machine called a shield machine that digs through the soil and rock little by little. The excavated materials are then removed from the tunnel by trolley cars, with concrete sprayed on the walls to prevent them from collapsing. However, the civil engineering technology at the time made it difficult to use the shield-tunneling method for tunnels with an inner diameter as much as 9 meters, a view shared by most civil engineers. In fact, while Hatta was in North America, the first question he asked in Albany at the headquarters of the American Society of Civil Engineers was whether or not to use this method. He was told it was too risky. The first tunnel to be constructed in Japan using the shield-tunneling method was the Kanmon Undersea Tunnel, which did not begin until 1936.

In order to make a final confirmation, Hatta asked Fujie, who was to be in charge of the tunnel construction site for the Okura Civil Engineering Corporation, to make a trip to inspect the Tanna Tunnel site and meet with those in charge of the construction there. When Fujie returned from his trip, he told Hatta that while the shield-tunneling method was the best for a tunnel with a diameter of 4 to 5 meters, the engineers involved in the Tanna Tunnel thought that the risk of using that method was too great for a tunnel with a diameter of nearly 10 meters.

Hatta and Fujie walked around the Wushanling site many times. It was physically challenging, as the air was thick with virgin forest and high humidity, and sweat was pouring out of them, which could make them lose consciousness. The two of them were silent. After much thought, Hatta decided to abandon hopes for using the shield-tunnel method and to go with the traditional method.

The groundbreaking ceremony for the Wushanling Tunnel was held on June 8, 1922. Steam excavators, steam locomotives, air dump trucks, and giant pumps for the dam, rock drills, underground shovels, and air compressors for tunnel excavation had already been purchased through a leading U.S. civil engineering and construction machinery manufacturer. These were transported one after another, via Keelung Port and Kaohsiung Port to Banzida Station by the North-South Railway, and from there to Wushantou Station by the newly laid light railroad.

Figure 4.5   Air Dump Car Dropping Rocks and Fill. *Source*: (from Wu, Kanan Taishū Kensetsu Kōtei Kankai)

There had been the question of how to transport the heavy machinery to Wushantou, and this is where the expertise of the Okura staff came in handy. Fujie proposed the construction of a 24-kilometer overhead road and a "ropeway," as it was called at the time, from Wushantou to the lower and upper reaches of the river. This was approved by Hatta. The proposed ropeway was thick enough to withstand a weight of 24 tons. Hatta imagined rock drills and underground shovels being lifted into the air and moving effortlessly. He became excited that he was getting closer to making the project a reality.

The tunnel was excavated simultaneously from both the upper and lower reaches of Wushanling. The reason for this was to shorten the construction period as much as possible. Three shafts were excavated at the same time, each with a diameter of several meters, to form a horseshoe-shaped tunnel. The tunnels were sprayed with concrete from a mixing machine to protect them from earth pressure and spring water. The excavated rock was carried out of the tunnel on a trolley by an underground shovel. Where there was a risk of the concrete collapsing by the strong pressure from above, pine logs brought in from Japan were used to prop up the walls and prevent it from happening. It was simple work, but it required a lot of patience.

ETERNAL HELL

The main shaft, a horseshoe of 9 meters in diameter, was excavated to a depth of about 50 meters from the tunnel entrance. Hatta gave Fujie words of encouragement, predicting that if the tunnel were bored at this rate at intervals of 40 to 50 meters, the excavation of a total length of 3,109 meters would be a success. However, on December 6, 1922, a gas explosion occurred about 80 meters from the entrance of the downstream section of the tunnel.

Hatta received the news of the explosion by telephone while working in his office in Wushantou. He was incredulous and raced as fast as he could by horse to the site.

Catching his breath upon arrival, Hatta could hear people screaming and sobbing at the entrance of the tunnel. "Damn it. What should not have been allowed to happen, happened, out of carelessness."

Fujie told him that at least fifty people had been killed: some were operating rock drills in loincloths, some were drilling holes, some were removing rocks by trolley, and some were spraying concrete walls when the explosion happened. The blackened corpses were carried out one after another on stretchers. The smell of burned human flesh filled the tunnel.

Hatta entered the tunnel with its repugnant smell and proceeded to the explosion area. Charred corpses were being carried out by their colleagues and fellow laborers. Five dismembered bodies were strewn about and black pieces of flesh stuck to the walls of the tunnel as if nearly evaporated by the blast. It was like Hell. Hatta felt defeated.

Men with blackened faces were picking up the pieces of their fellow workers and collecting them by trolley. Most of them escaped death, but many were seriously injured. The wounded were taken by stretcher to a hospital in Chiayi under the direction of Fujie, the construction supervisor.

The corpses lying at the mouth of the tunnel and the lumps of flesh whose names could not be determined were collected on top of straw mats and covered. Families living in the villages of Wushantou carried babies on their shoulders or pulled young children by the hand as they searched for their husbands and fathers, pale and helpless. The cries turned to sobs, and Hatta could do nothing but hang his head low.

That night, Hatta went back to the Wushantou Office for a while. He was so sad that he could hardly contain himself. Hatta was overcome by a deep sense of disappointment that he had never experienced in his life. He had been in a daze for about two hours. Sometime after seeing the pale morning light rise in Wushantou, he rode his horse back to the accident site.

The laborers had already gathered and finished sorting out the corpses and pieces of flesh. Those whose identity were known had their names written on white cotton cloths that were placed on the bodies, while those whose names were unknown were silently being searched for any personal belongings to help identify them. Amid the strong smell of death, Hatta checked each body, offered incense, knelt in front of the corpse, and laid his hand on it in silence.

He thought to himself that he had to investigate the cause of the accident before all else. He must repeatedly offer his condolences to the bereaved families. Hatta had no choice but to go forward. He cooperated with local police to conduct the accident investigation.

A mountain is made up of many layers of strata. Clay, sand, and rocks of various sizes form layers that rise to the surface due to crustal movement and volcanic activity, and eventually become mountains. Tunneling is the process of digging through multiple layers of strata. The type and strength of excavators and drills are adjusted for each stratum.

A fracture zone is a band of rock that has been shattered by long-term fault movement. These are regularly encountered. Fracture zones are often mixed with groundwater. When they came to a fracture zone, high-pressure water would erupt along with the crushed rocks. Hatta was well aware of this fact.

What he was unaware of, however, was the existence of the oil shale formation, now widely known as "oil shale." As the name implies, the rock formation contains flammable oil. When the rock drills were 80 meters from the tunnel mouth, they struck the largest oil shale formation they had ever experienced, and a large amount of oil gas erupted. At that moment, the gas ignited the construction lanterns, causing them to flash, and with a roar, they burst into flames. This explosion killed or injured the workers nearby or in the tunnel. Five workers were totally blown apart by the instantaneous thermal expansion. Body parts, even skeletons of the victims, were unidentifiable.

Hatta, together with the geological experts of Okura Civil Engineering Corporation, began a thorough review of the tunnel strata. The oil shale layer was limited to a 2-meter-wide layer about 80 meters from the tunnel mouth. It was also determined that most of the built-up energy had been released due to the gas blowout, and the construction work could be restarted. Hatta informed directors Yamagata and Shimomura of the full details of the accident and its cause and rejected the argument of some in the governor-general's office that the design should be changed. The accident occurred in December 1922 and, confident that the reasons for the accident were understood and that there was little likelihood that it would happen again, construction was restarted in early 1923.

THE ORIGIN OF "HATTA DAM"

The construction of the Wushantou Dam resumed. The clay, dirt, and rocks found in Dainaisho, a tributary of the Sobun River, were loaded onto large shovels, lifted onto air dump trucks waiting on the newly laid railroad, and transported to Wushantou 20 kilometers away. The rails were two lanes, permitting roundtrips. Twenty air dump trucks at a time were connected to the steam locomotive. The locomotive exhaled black smoke as it rumbled through the quiet fields and forests. To the farmers watching this scene, it must have seemed like a tsunami running on land.

When work began, Hatta road on top of a load of rocks, excited to be part of this wild procession of vehicles. Hatta took off his hat and waved it to waving farmers. Hatta felt emboldened.

As soon as they arrived at the planned site at Wushantou, the air compressed by the steam tilted the carriage and the fully loaded clay, sand, rocks, and boulders crashed down onto the two weirs being constructed with a resounding thud. This simple work went on and on, rain or shine.

At the same time, they had to construct a reinforced concrete core barrier in the center of the two weirs. The reinforced concrete core, 3.64 meters high, 1.54 meters wide at the base, and 0.91 meters wide at the top, was placed vertically above the base of the Neogene layer.

This was literally the core, located in the center of the trapezoidal dam after its completion, and a large amount of clay is stretched over this core to become the central layer of the most important barrier wall.

The clay, gravel, and rocks brought to the dam from the connected air dump trucks are broken down, and the water drawn from the Guantian River is sprayed over the broken soil with five giant pumps. This was done a mind-boggling number of times. In the meantime, the two dams were made up of clay, then silt, sand, pebbles, and rocks, which were drawn into the center to form a single weir.

The water that flowed down had to be drained. Hatta had designed a drainage culvert just below the clay layer barrier wall surrounding the central concrete core, and two more drainage culverts excavated at the bottom of the sand filter layer on either side of the barrier wall, to drain into the Guantian River outside the weir. The filter layer is a literal filter composed of sand. The design was that through this filter layer, water would flow out of the dam in large quantities through culverts.

Joel Justin, an authority on civil engineering in the United States, was asked by the governor-general's office to point out any problems with the Wushantou Dam, which also proceeded as designed, and he visited the site and had discussions with Hatta. Justin agreed that the Wushantou Dam should proceed as planned by Hatta. However, Justin pointed out to the Public Works Bureau that if an issue had to be identified, he felt that the central concrete core was too low, which could lead to incomplete imperviousness.

In Hatta's opinion, if the central concrete core is too high in earthquake-prone Taiwan, there was a risk of the core cracking during earthquakes, which

Figure 4.6   Concrete Core of Dam Being Filled. *Source*: (from Wu, Kanan Taishū Kensetsu Kōtei Kankai)

could cause the dam to collapse. When the water level of the dam rises, the groundwater level inside the dam also rises, and the water saturation inside the dam reaches its limit, the high concrete core would be subjected to strong pressure and crack, which could cause the dam to collapse. This was what Hatta was afraid of. The water infiltrating the dam would not be blocked by the high concrete core, but rather led to the drainage culverts directly underneath and on either side of the low concrete core to let the water out of the dam. Hatta's original idea was that this would maintain the stability of the embankment.

In fact, for this purpose, Hatta measured the amount of water seeping into the dam at different locations many times. Justin eventually agreed with Hatta's argument and, on the condition that Hatta submit the subsequent progress of the water seepage to the American Society of Civil Engineers from time to time, he agreed to Hatta's concept in its entirety and returned to the United States. It was for this reason that the Wushantou Dam would later become known as the "Hatta Dam" within the American Society of Civil Engineers.

The fountains of high-water pressure from the giant pumps on either side of the central concrete core constantly poured clay and sand into the center of the dam between the two weirs, which had been made about 200 meters apart. The clay layers were finally joined at the central concrete core to form a single strong clay layer.

CAPABLE MEN LAID OFF

After the completion of the dam, the eighty staff members of the Public Works Bureau had been mobilized to prepare an overall plan for the waterway system to ensure that the water released from the dam would be able to reach the entire Chianan Plain, but they were not sure if the water would actually flow through the region as planned. Hatta left the dam project to his subordinate, Isoda Norio, and turned his attention to the Chianan Irrigation System project.[2]

It was on December 6, 1922, that the gas explosion in the Wushanling Tunnel occurred, putting Hatta in a tight spot. The following year, on September 1, 1923, he received the news that the Great Kantō Earthquake had struck Tokyo. Once again, Hatta was put in a difficult position.

The death toll was large and the cost of rebuilding the Imperial capital was enormous. The earthquake would no doubt have an impact governor-general's office in Taiwan. It was only natural for the governor-general's office to offer reconstruction assistance to the government, and the financial support it provided amounted to one-third of the governor-general's office's annual budget. The governor-general was forced to reduce various budgets and subsidies to make up for the lack of funds. The budget for the construction of Chianan Irrigation System was no exception.

The governor-general's office had to postpone some of the construction work and make every effort to reduce costs, and then use the remaining funds to carry out the work for that and other projects.

Hatta was directed to liquidate about half of the association's members working for him. Since the head of the Wushantou Sub-branch Office had been given the authority to hire staff, Hatta had no choice but to be the one responsible for the layoffs. Hatta, who had been entrusted with the front line of the Chianan Irrigation System project, was tempted to curse the cruel fate he found himself in less than a year after the gas explosion in the tunnel had claimed the lives of fifty people. However, what had to be done had to be done.

Hatta knew very well that his staff and the laborers were troubled by what was going on. He consulted with his subordinate Yamane Chōjirō, but he was unable to come up with a good idea. After much deliberation, Hatta decided on a drastic plan to deal with laying off half of the staff and laborers.

Resentment would grow among those who were fired, and an emotional rift would be created between them and those who were not fired. This rift had to be avoided at all costs if the construction were to continue. Here is what Hatta did: he gathered the heads of each section of employees to the Wushantou Office and had them present their evaluations of the performance of each employee. For those whose evaluations were unclear as to how accurate they were, Hatta met with each group leader to discuss the specific cases and decided, counterintuitively, to let go those who scored highly, while giving them bonuses, and to retain those who scored poorly.

Hatta stunned everyone with this approach, but he had his reasons. He felt that those who had performed well would be able to find employment even if they left Wushantou, but those who had not performed well could not easily find work and should be allowed to stay on at Wushantou. In this way, those that were retained would work harder. And for those who laid off, Hatta and his staff would try to find employment for them with the companies involved in the construction of the Wushantou Dam and Wushanling Tunnel, as well as through Hatta's own personal contacts. When construction work resumed in full, Hatta promised to give priority to rehiring those who had been laid off.

Although the construction period had to be extended due to the Great Kantō Earthquake, the work itself proceeded mainly with the construction of the water supply channel. The original plan was to start construction in September 1920 and finish in March 1926, a six-year project, but Hatta was forced to extend the construction period by four years to a ten-year plan.

In the meantime, Hatta continued to insist to the governor-general's office that financing and reduction of the burden of association members should be approved by all means. In the end, he was able to obtain an increase in the total construction budget and a four-year government subsidy. Hatta was moved to tears at his success in convincing Yamagata and Shimomura, and the governor-general office's efforts to persuade the central government in Tokyo. Above all, the construction of the Chianan Irrigation System was a great effort for the people of Taiwan and Japan. Hatta was deeply impressed by the fact that it was approved, and he was determined to devote all the energy he had left to the completion of the Chianan Irrigation System.

Nine months had passed since the Great Kantō Earthquake, and a new vigor had returned to Chianan Irrigation System project. However, Hatta felt that the quality of the new energy was different from the old one. Perhaps it was because everyone now shared the same sense of national pride in the Wushantou Dam and the importance of this project to the governor-general's office, which had led to the full resumption of construction after the oil gas explosion in the tunnel, the budget reductions after the earthquake, and the forced layoffs.

NOTES

1. Kōkyō Hishū Kanan Taishū Kumiai, *Kōkyō Hishū Kanan Taishū Shinsetsu Jigyō Gaiyō* (Outline of the Public Waterworks Chianan Irrigation New Construction Project), 1930, located in Kōeki Zaidan Hōjin Doboku Gakkai Doboku Jinbutsu

Aakaibusu Hatta Yoichi Kanren Shiryō (Hatta Yoichi Related Materials in the Archives of People of the Japan Society of Civil Engineers).

2. See Furukawa Katsumi, *Taiwan o Aishita Nihonjin: Hatta Yoichi no Shōgai* (A Japanese Man Who Loved Taiwan: The Life of Hatta Yoichi) (Tokyo: Sōfūsha, 2009), and Hokkoku Shimbunsha Shuppankyoku, ed., *Kaisō no Hatta Yoichi: Ichikazoku Ya Yukari no Hito no Shōgen de Tsuzuru* (Reflections of Hatta Yoichi: Family and Those with a Connection Remember Him) (Kanazawa: Hokkoku Shimbunsha, 2016).

Chapter 5

Why the Chianan Irrigation System Succeeded

THE CHIANAN PLAIN BECAME A SHEET OF GREEN

Engineer Hatta Yoichi and his team next had to put all their efforts into completing the water supply system. With the Zhuoshui River, the construction of the three water intakes was completed. From the intakes, the water from the Zhuoshui River system would be led through a waterway to the main water supply channel called the Zhuoshui Trunk Line.

The water released from the north-south trunk line junction of the Wushantou Dam was directed northward to the North Trunk Line, on one side, and southward to the South Trunk Line, on the other side. The trunk line, combining the Zhuoshui Trunk Line, North Trunk Line, and South Trunk Line, is the largest water supply system for the Chianan Plain.

The North Trunk Line flows northward from the north-south trunk line junction at Wushantou to the Zhuoshui Trunk Line, crossing the Jishui River, Bazhang River, and Puzi River. The water taken in from the Zhuoshui River intake becomes the Zhuoshui Trunk Line. The distance to Wushantou is forty-seven kilometers.

The South Trunk Line, which flows south from the Wushantou Dam, crosses the Zengwen River and divides into several branch lines at the end, where Tainan can be seen in the distance.

To the east of the three trunks line is the Alishan mountain range, which runs north to south through much of the length of Taiwan. It is a huge mountain massif with its northern end at Zhuoshui River and reaching as far south as Kaohsiung. The slopes on the east side of the mainline are steep. In contrast, the slopes on the west side are relatively gentle and gradually become less steep, leading to the vast Chianan Plain. Across the plain is the Taiwan Strait.

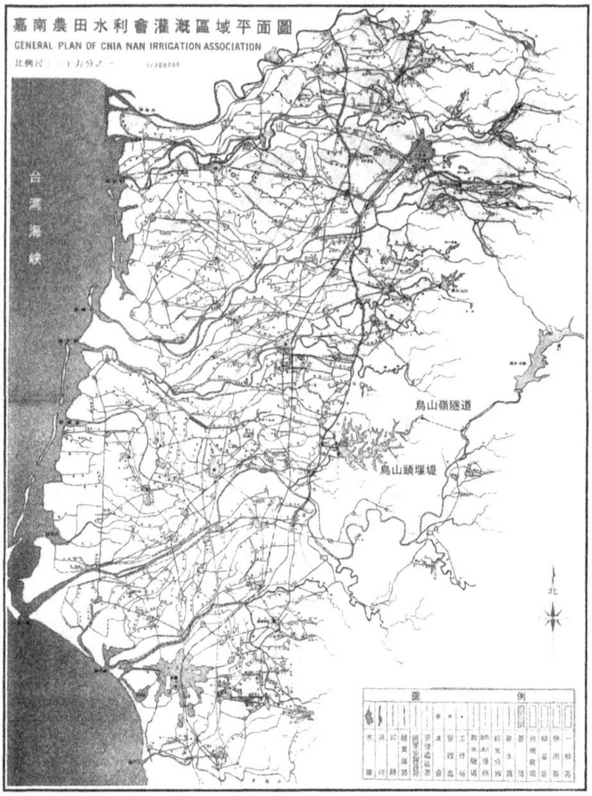

Figure 5.1   General Plan of Chianan Irrigation Association. *Source*: (from Wu, Kanan Taishū Kensetsu Kōtei Kankai)

Hatta sometimes rode a bicycle and sometimes a horse to explore the area along the northern and southern lines. In order to supply water equally to the entire 150,000-hectare Chianan Plain, a detailed gradient map of the Chianan Plain had to be created. The lifeline of both trunk lines and waterways is the gradient. It is necessary to survey every mainline, division line, and branch line. No matter how huge the dam is, it will be meaningless unless it can supply water to the fields evenly and widely.

A considerable number of staff and association members were devoted to the triangulation. Hatta appointed Akabori Shinichi, whom he trusted, as the supervisor. Akabori called the Wushantou Sub-branch Office every day to report the survey results. Hatta was able to draw the slope of the plains on the map on the desk of the sub-branch office in detail. He incorporated the topographical maps of each area into his mind and drew the entire slope structure of the plain in detail.

At the point where the southern main line crosses the Beigang River, the construction of the Puzi River Water Bridge was proceeding. Hatta took a break in that area and sat down on a hill near the bridge.

It was already autumn. The sun, which had been strong during the day, was no longer shining and was setting on Mt. Yu, or Jade Mountain, beyond the Alishan range. Alishan's main peak, Mt. Datashan, was quickly fading into the distance. Layers and layers of the mountain range turned jet black. If you look at the plains, the sky becomes more and more blue, and the whole plains glow with flowers. The evening stars were faintly shining. They headed back to the Wushantou Sub-branch Office in the dark by horse, the next day being an early one for them.

The North Trunk Line has to cross large rivers such as the Gueijong, Bazhang, and Puzi. A steel aqueduct supported by concrete piers was built to carry the water. The South Trunk Line also required three aqueducts: Guantian River, Duzhaitou River, and Zengwen River. They were squarish, steel pipes, about twice as tall as the people building them. From a distance, the structure could be mistaken for a railroad bridge.

The water released from the Wushantou Dam falls into a stillwater pond below the spillway, where it is decompressed, and flows slowly through a junction to both the north and south main lines. At the bifurcation point, a "tainter gate type sluice gate," was installed, which consisted of a number of iron fan-shaped wings to automatically stabilize the amount of water passing through. The distance of the North Trunk Line is about 500 kilometers, and the South Trunk Line is about 10 kilometers. The North Trunk Line runs northward from the junction point and connects with the Zhuoshui Trunk Line through a culvert.

The water released from the trunk line and flowing in the direction of the Taiwan Strait goes to the branch line, from the branch line to the diversion channel, from the diversion channel to the water supply channel, and then after irrigating the fields, it goes through the drainage channel and finally flows into the Taiwan Strait.

The volume of water stored in the Wushantou Dam is 150 million tons. The outlet of the Wushantou Dam is 63.5 meters above sea level.

The distance from the dam to the Taiwan Strait is only about 30 kilometers in a straight line. Without the layout of a 16,000 km long waterway on this short distance of plain, it would be impossible to equally distribute water to 150,000 hectares of arable land.

The work of meticulously mapping out the gradients of the trunk lines, branch lines, and water supply channels was extremely detailed, and the depth and width of the waterways had to be meticulously studied to take advantage of slight slopes.

COMPLETION OF THE WUSHANTOU DAM

The strong winds blowing across the Taiwan Strait to the Chianan Plain caused seawater to affect the soil. When the wave caps break up at sea, saltwater droplets are scattered in the air, which are then carried by the wind and landing on arable land in some places. The scale of salt damage is even greater if the soil is washed away by strong wind waves at high tide. If the soil accumulates too much salt, crops will not grow. The only way to prevent salt damage is to build a seawall to dam up the intrusion of seawater. Hatta remembered that there was a method called the "automatic tide stopper drainage gate" for this purpose, and after reading a lot of literature on this method, he decided to use it.

The gate was designed to automatically close at high tide to prevent seawater from entering and to open at low tide to allow water from the drainage channel to flow out toward the Strait. The arrangement of the twenty rows of sluice gates, with their concrete perimeters firmly in place, was awe-inspiring. The total length of the project was ninety-six kilometers, and it was constructed in twenty-five locations along the Taiwan Strait.

In order to construct such major works as the Wushantou Dam and the Wushanling Tunnel using large civil engineering machines, electric energy was indispensable. In particular, in order to make up for the extended construction period forced by the Great Kantō Earthquake, it was inevitable to work both day and night. The first plan was to generate electricity by using the rapids of the Zhuoshui River. Focusing on the abundance of water in the conduit channel leading from the intake of the Zhuoshui River, a generator was installed there.

The completion of the Wushantou Dam was already in Hatta's mind. He marked the completed sections on the map of the Chianan Plain on the wall in his office, and as he watched the marks gradually become denser and denser, he realized that the completion date was steadily approaching.

By this time, all that remained of the Wushantou Dam was the construction of the water outlet and the water delivery port.

The water taken in from the intake passes through a water transmission tunnel in the dam, and the amount of water transmitted is controlled by two butterfly valves installed in the tunnel. The tunnel branches off again inside the dam, and the water is released outside the dam through a total of five outlets.

Even if the water in the dam increased due to heavy rainfall, the amount of water stored in the dam had to be kept constant. This is because there was the risk that the dam would be damaged by the strong water pressure inside of it. A water storage draft line was set at 40 meters, and if the water level rose above that level, a belt-shaped water outlet was completed to automatically release water from the top of the dam to the outside.

Figure 5.2   Wushantou Dam in Operation. *Source*: (from Wu, Kanan Taishū Kensetsu Kōtei Kankai)

The Wushantou Dam was completed on May 10, 1930, with a total length of 1,273 meters, a bank height of 56 meters, and a storage capacity of 150.1 million tons when full. The Hoover Dam, located on the border of the U.S. states of Arizona and Nevada and named after the then president Herbert Hoover, was completed in 1936. Until the completion of the Hoover Dam, the Wushantou Dam was the largest of its kind in the world.

The completion ceremony was held on May 10, 1930, with the participation of 3,000 Japanese and 600 Taiwanese people, and a grand celebration was held for three weeks. In the middle of the celebration events, the water pumping ceremony was held at the Wushantou Dam. Many people were moved to tears, wiping their eyes, as all the water outlets were opened, and the water roared for the first time. Unable to conceal his own feelings, Hatta, now forty-four years old, watched the flow of water from the water outlet to the water conduit full of pride at his and his team's work.

EPOCH-MAKING USE OF THE "THREE-FIELD SYSTEM"

There is a farming method known as the "three-field system."[1] It is believed to have developed in Europe during the Middle Ages, but it is also used in arid regions of southwest Asia and northwest India, where it is difficult to obtain water for irrigation. The entire arable land of a village is divided into three parts, one of which is planted with spring-sown grains, the other with autumn-sown grains, and the remaining part is left fallow for grazing live-stock. This process is repeated every year, alternating fields, so that it takes three years to complete a cycle of cultivation. The three-field system is a farming method that allows livestock to graze after the harvest of both spring and fall sown grains, conserves water through fallowing, and at the same time maintains the fertility of the arable land.

Hatta had been familiar with this farming method since his university days. The uniqueness of Hatta's idea lies in the fact that he connected this three-field system to the water supply in the Chianan Plain. It was an epoch-making effort. Initially, Hatta called it the "cyclical irrigation system" and later the "three-year rotation water supply system."

The Chianan Plain covers an area of 150,000 hectares. The large plain was divided into "water supply zones" in a careful layout with a standard unit of about 150 hectares. The total number of water supply zones in the Chianan Plain therefore numbered about 10,000. Each of the 10,000 water supply plots was divided into three sections again, and each year the water was sup-plied in a cyclical manner.

The irrigation of rice was from May to October in the water supply area using the Zhuoshui Trunk Line as the main water source and from June to September in the water supply area using the south and north trunk lines as the main water sources. This is the first year.

For the sweet crop, the irrigation period is from the end of the rice crop to March of the following year, which is the second year. After each irrigation is completed, water is supplied to the miscellaneous crop water supply areas until March or April of the second year, and then to the third year.

After the first year's water supply, the rice plots will be left fallow, fol-lowed by the sweet crop plots, which will also be left fallow. The same is true for miscellaneous crops. By taking a long fallow period, the water supply is limited, and the fertility preserved, thus making it possible to supply water throughout the Chianan Plain.

If the farmers did not initially understand the three-year crop rotation water supply method, they would not be able to cooperate. Nakajima Rikio, who was appointed to be in charge of the waterway construction, made every effort to design the end of the waterway system while patiently explaining the advan-tages of this water supply method to each farmer. He carefully studied the slope of the water supply system, and based on the results, he thoroughly instructed the farmers and completed a nearly horizontal waterway system. When he tried to test the water supply, he found that water flowed through all the channels from the main line to the end. In fact, it took three days. Nakashima was moved to tears when he saw the joy on the faces of the farmers as they watched the thin stream of water flowing through the rain-fed rice paddy fields for the first time.

This method of farming increased the area of arable land, as well as the production of paddy rice and sweet crops, and increased the unit yield. Furthermore, the land price, which had been almost worthless because of the lack of productivity of the fields, rose, greatly benefiting the farmers. The measurements that prove this are found in the *Outline of the Chianan Irrigation New Construction Project.*

This project made it possible to introduce Hōrai Rice to the Chianan Plains. As introduced in chapter 2, born as "Taichū 65 Gō" and developed by Iso Eikichi, Suenaga Megumu, and others, Hōrai Rice was established as a pure rice and was introduced to Taipei, Hsinchu, and the Chianan Plains, the largest rice field in Taiwan. The entire plain became a sea of green of Hōrai Rice. Hatta was stunned by the sight of fields usually suffering during the dry

Figure 5.3   3-Crop Rotation System. *Source*: (from Taihoku Beikoku Jimusho, ed. Kanan Taishū: Beikoku Jimusho Chōsa, p. 115 (1936))

season or destroyed by flooding. This was a dramatic transformation of the Chianan Plain.

The construction of the lateral canal, branch lines, water supply channels, and drainage channels were all done by the Water Supply Association. The guidance of farmers was also essential for the new agricultural method of dividing the water supply into separate plots to promote the three-year crop rotation water supply method. This guidance and dissemination were carried out under the direction of the governor-general's office.

It was the landowners, including small farmers, who were organized as agricultural associations that were directly responsible for rice and sweet crop cultivation. The creativity and motivation of the individual farmers were put to good use here.

The design of infrastructure was the exclusive responsibility of the governor-general's office, but it was the farmers themselves who worked hard toward its construction and agricultural production. Mutual competition for greater crop yields resulted in higher yields. Already at this point, Japan had introduced the system into Taiwan in which the public and private sectors were separated but the public sector helped the private sector with major infrastructure and production was raised by the mutual competition within the private sector.

It is not a coincidence that Hōrai Rice was not born by chance. It was an improved variety that Iso and Suenaga had finally created after an infinite number of crossbreeding attempts. In order to grow the rice there, level arable land needed to be created, irrigation was needed from the water source, seedlings had to be prepared, they had to be transferred to the field and fertilized. Only after this could the rice be harvested after growing.

Fertilization is an absolute must. The rice must be "sensitized" to the fertilizer applied, and only then can high yields be obtained. This is why conventional farming methods that are unable to use water from irrigation and do not apply fertilizer are called "coarse farming," while farming that uses water from irrigation to increase the effectiveness of fertilizer application is called "intensive farming." The introduction of Hōrai Rice meant a shift from coarse farming to intensive farming. The same principle applies to sweet crop cultivation as well.

The conversion of fertilizer-free agriculture to fertilizer-intensive agriculture will naturally increase costs. In Japan, chemical fertilizers such as soybean meal from Manchuria and sometimes potash from Germany were used. However, fertilizers were not used in Taiwan's agriculture up to that time. Farmers just threw in paddy grains, straw, grass ash, and burned earth.

The improved variety called Hōrai Rice had to be introduced to the farmers at all costs, but the question was how to get the farmers to use chemical fertilizers if they were concerned about the increased cost that fertilizer entailed.

Hatta gave it some thought and decided to distribute fertilizer free of charge at first. He did so as well for the sweet crops. This was to make the farmers understand that the new farming method would lead to higher profits. The next step was to provide subsidies for the purchase of fertilizer, and then the farmers' association would jointly purchase the fertilizer and distribute it to the farmers, and finally the farmers would bear the cost of the fertilizer themselves. This turned out to be a reasonable approach.

In the Chianan Plain, the simple yield of Hōrai Rice clearly increased, and the net income, even after deducting the cost of fertilizer purchased, had risen in almost every area. At the time Hatta was making his best efforts as the director of the Wushantou Sub-branch Office, the Chianan Plain Administration Organization had been reorganized by the governor-general's office as the "Public Waterworks Chianan Irrigation System Association." The plain began to function in a coordinated manner, with the many smaller farmers' associations coming under an umbrella organization. The membership rules read as follows:

Article 2: The association is an organization for those landowners, pledgees, tenants, and reservoir/waterway owners with a stake in Public Waterworks Chianan Irrigation System.

Article 3: The purpose of this association is to maintain the land and water utilization facilities of Public Waterworks Chianan Irrigation System.[2]

Under these regulations, the interested parties in the Chianan Plain consisted of landowners, pledgees, tenants, and reservoir/waterway owners. A pledgee is a person who lends land, money, or goods to another person and is the owner of the security interest or collateral.

The water supply and drainage projects in Chianan Irrigation System, the introduction of the three-year crop rotation water supply method, the mobilization of labor for the construction of water supply and drainage channels, and the payment of construction costs were mostly covered by the "water tax" (water use tax) paid by the farmers' association for use of the irrigation system. The members of the farmers' association were elected by its members.

In the popular imagination, Japan was the ruler of Taiwan, and Japan was represented in Taiwan by the governor-general's office, with the governor-general himself being all powerful, like an "emperor." In reality, this was not the case. The fact that administration was managed by autonomous units such as the water users' association and the farmers' association of interested parties shows the rational and decentralized nature of Japan's rule over Taiwan.

ESTABLISHMENT OF THE MEMORIAL
TO THE 134 WHO DIED

The Wushanling Tunnel, the most challenging project in the Chianan Irrigation System, was penetrated on June 17, 1928, and the surrounding facilities were completed on November 12 of the same year.

The Wushantou Dam was completed on May 10, 1930. On May 15, a huge discharge of water was released from the dam's outlet into the conduit pool. Everyone gathered around the spillway, cheering and congratulating Hatta.

It is interesting that people who have accomplished a great task become so quiet at such times. Hatta stared at the roaring water flowing from the outlet to the north-south trunk line via the water conduit without speaking. It was a strange sense of listlessness that he could not quite explain, not quite a sense of accomplishment or satisfaction. He probably first thought of the Japanese and Taiwanese workers who died during the construction.

From the start of construction to the completion of the project, Hatta wondered how many people had devoted themselves to this huge project under his direction. In the midst of the construction work, such feelings did not come to mind.

By the time the completion ceremony finally arrived, Hatta felt like hanging his head in awe of the dedication of his subordinates. From the beginning of the construction until just before the completion, Hatta often looked at the photos that people had taken and given to him. He was moved by them. There was one, for example, of most of the engineers from the old days gathered at the groundbreaking ceremony of the Wushantou Reservoir and its spillway on February 16, 1929. In it, to Hatta's right sitting in the front row, was his eldest son, Akio, who was still very young.

The completion of the Chianan Irrigation System was just around the corner, and Hatta was going to move to Taipei in the near future, having been appointed as the chief of the Water Supply Section, Civil Engineering Department, Home Affairs Bureau of the governor-general's office. After the completion of the construction, he planned to erect a "monument to the fallen workers" as a sign of repose for the souls of those who died during the construction. In March 1930, the monument was completed.

The names of the 134 victims, both Japanese and Taiwanese, were engraved on three sides of the foundation stone supporting the tall monument in the chronological order of their deaths. Having thought carefully about what he wished inscribed, Hatta added the following on the fourth side of the foundation stone:

The Chianan Plain is world-renowned for the vastness of the land stretching East, West, North, and South from which the area benefits as well as for its magnificent water source construction methods. The construction method was extremely precise, and despite the many difficulties encountered during the construction process, the project was finally completed after ten years of hard work. During this time, many of those engaged in the work suffered from unforeseen calamities and endemic diseases and were laid to rest in a cemetery away from home. It is truly regrettable. However, all of them were martyrs with a strong sense of sacrifice, who risked their lives to inspire their employees, and thus were able to contribute to the eventual completion of this massive project. It is truly a great achievement. The water from the Zengwen River, flowing like an undulating stream, will fill the dam forever and through that irrigate the fields forever. In this, the names of those men who died will be immortalized. We have chosen this place to erect this monument here with words inscribed to share for future generations the honor of those who died.

The day had come for Hatta to leave Wushantou. In August 1930, he and Toyoki, his eldest daughter, Masako, his eldest son, Akio, his second son, Yasuo, his second daughter, Ayako, his third daughter, Hiroko, his fourth daughter, Yoshiko, his fifth daughter, Reiko, and his sixth daughter, Shigeko, who was still in her mother's womb and would be born at the end of the year, moved to the governor-general's office's housing area in Taipei.

The new governor-general's office building had not yet been built, but about 1 kilometer west of the proposed site was Saiwai-chō, where many Japanese people lived. There were churches, schools, and commercial facilities, and the streets were neat and tidy, and Hatta was able to find some peace.

He was now forty-four years old. He came to Taiwan upon graduating from the Civil Engineering Department of the Tokyo Imperial College of Technology and became an engineer in the Civil Engineering Department of the governor-general's office in 1910, when he was twenty-four years old. So, twenty years had passed since then. Ever since he got the idea for the irrigation project in the Chianan Plain, he had devoted all his energy to the construction of tunnels, dams, and water supply channels in the plains, and he had never enjoyed a moment's rest.

Hatta's new position was chief of the Water Supply Section, Civil Engineering Department, Home Affairs Bureau. This may seem like a low position for Hatta, but he was a high ranking official. His rank was higher than his job title. At that time, there were four ranks: *shinninkan* (minister, etc.), *chokuninkan* (vice minister, etc.), *sōninkan* (director), *hanninkan* (special civil servant). The highest rank was given only to the governor-general, and only the directors of the Home Bureau were given the imperial appointment. Hatta was the only engineer to be given the honor of an imperial appointment, which was granted to him in recognition of his outstanding achievements in leading the Chianan Irrigation System to success.

At the time, there were 488 engineers in the Civil Engineering Division of the Home Affairs Bureau, Hatta's main workplace. Hatta's official rank was higher than that of his boss, the head of the Civil Engineering Division. Hatta stood at the top of the engineers in the governor-general's office.

THE ENGINEERS' GROUP, WARRIORS FOR DEVELOPING THE SOUTHERN AREAS

Unfortunately, this time—the 1930s—also saw the march toward war globally, once again. After the Japanese occupation of southern Indochina in July 1941, the U.S. government froze Japanese assets in the United States and banned all oil exports to Japan, making the outbreak of hostilities between the two countries almost inevitable. The United Kingdom, China, and the Netherlands followed the United States, and the so-called ABCD line by American, British, Chinese, and the Dutch, was undertaken.

In June of the same year, the Japanese government, sensing the formation of this encirclement in advance, announced the "Outline of Measures against the Southern Areas" with the aim of "promptly expanding the comprehensive national defense capability for the Empire's self-preservation and self-defense. To this end, a group of "Personnel for Industrial Development in the Southern Areas" was formed by the five ministries of the army, navy, colonial affairs, commerce and industry, and agriculture and forestry. The technicians specialized in a wide range of fields, including petroleum, mining, sugar refining, oils and fats, textiles, agriculture, water supply, fisheries, and cattle breeding. The number of dispatched personnel was about 1,000, selected by the five ministries, and there was no distinction between the public and private sectors.

In response to a request from the Philippine Military Command, the Army's Military Administration Department, through the governor-general's office in Taiwan, approached Hatta in 1942 after the war broke out to dispatch him to the Philippines to lead the Cotton Crop Irrigation Project.

Hatta agreed to go. He was also told to recommend some experts to accompany him. Hatta was proud that his achievements had been recognized and that he had been given a chance to utilize his experience in the Chianan Irrigation System project outside of Taiwan. He also thought that this was a good opportunity for the talented engineers under him to gain experience in other countries and refine their skills. The faces of Miyaji Suehiko, Yumoto Masao, and Ichikawa Matsutarō immediately came to mind, and when he invited them, they were all eager to participate.

After graduating from the former Kanazawa First Junior High School and the Fourth Senior High School, Miyaji majored in agricultural civil engineering at the Tokyo Imperial University, and upon graduation from the university in 1931, went to work for the governor-general's office in Taiwan. Although he was about ten years younger than Hatta, he had a similar background. He was instrumental in Hatta's vision of building water harvesting facilities in the Chianan Plain and popularizing the three-year crop rotation water supply method. He looked up to Hatta as his mentor and worked closely with him, and Hatta also relied on Miyaji.

After greeting the staff of the Public Works Bureau of the governor-general's office, Hatta took the three of them from Taipei to Keelung, where they boarded a large ship of the NYK Line, crossed the rough sea caused by a low-pressure system approaching the Taiwan Strait, and landed at Kobe in fine weather on April 21, 1942. They arrived in Tokyo around noon on April 22, having ridden the Tōkaidō Line's limited express train "Tsubame" and seeing the divine Mt. Fuji, which was heavily snow-capped, from the car's window on the left side. The weekend before, on April 18, 1942, Tokyo had been hit by the first air raid of B-25 bombers, the so-called Doolittle Raid.

Hatta and his men arrived in Tokyo four days after the raid, but there was not yet a tense atmosphere in Japan concerning the war. This would not come until June, when the U.S. military defeated Japanese forces at the Battle of Midway and begin their slow-but-steady counterattack in the Pacific. Until then, Japan had won all of its encounters and the victorious mood continued.

For Hatta and his men, there were no official duties until May 5, when they were to gather at Ujina Port in Hiroshima Prefecture and depart for the Philippines. They agreed to meet again on May 3 at the Tōkaidō Line ticket gate of Tokyo Station and went their separate ways for the next ten days. A sense of freedom filled Hatta's body for the first time in a long time, and he decided to stay at his cousin's house.

On April 23, he went to the Tokyo branch office of the Taiwan governor-general's office and then visited the Military Affairs Department of the Ministry of the Army in Ichigaya.

Two days earlier, he had read in the newspaper that Satō Kenryō, who was from his hometown, had been appointed director general of the Military Affairs Bureau of the Ministry of the Army, and he decided to go congratulate him on his appointment. Satō, who was nine years younger than Hatta, was a genuine soldier who had graduated from Kanazawa First Junior High School and then went on to the Imperial Japanese Army Academy and the Army War College. While not especially close, they knew each other's faces.

Because Satō had just been appointed to the post, he was away from the office paying calls on military and government officials. When he was told of Satō's absence, Hatta wrote only "Congratulations on your appointment as Director General of the Military Affairs Bureau of the Ministry of the Army" in the upper left-hand space of his business card, which read "Hatta

Yoichi, Imperial Engineer, Governor-General's Office, Taiwan," and told Satō's secretary to leave it on his desk in the director's office. He then left Ichigaya.

Hatta next went to the Ministry of Colonial Affairs, which was in charge of Taiwan, Korea, Manchuria, Sakhalin, and other "foreign lands" of Japan. The ministry was handling the affairs of their assignment to the Philippines. Hatta visited the office in Kodaira, where he was given an overview of the Philippine cotton crop and provided materials on water use in the Philippines in general.

Hatta's eldest son, Akio, who was born in Taipei, moved to Tokyo after graduating from Taipei First Junior High School, and was enrolled in the Faculty of Engineering at Tokyo Imperial University after attending the First High School in Tokyo. Hatta wanted to see Akio again after a long time, but his son was practicing with the university's rowing club and staying at the boathouse in Mukojima, and thus did not seem to have time.

Akio did show up at the cousin's house on the night of April 26. Hatta was relieved to see his tanned face. Accompanied by his cousin, his wife, and their two children, they had a reunion drink at a nearby sushi restaurant and Hatta gave him some spending money. Akio left for Mukojima immediately after dinner. That was the last time Hatta would see his beloved oldest son.

His eldest daughter, Masako, who, too, was born in Taipei, was also living in Tokyo. Masako was married to Fukao Tatsuo, a lecturer at the former Kanazawa Medical University. After retiring from the university, Fukao opened a hospital in Itabashi, Tokyo. The day after he met Akio, Hatta visited Masako, who had just given birth to her second child. Takashi was the first grandchild for Hatta and a very cute baby. Hatta stayed at his daughter's house that night.

While in Tokyo, Hatta also wanted to visit the Ogouchi Dam in Okutama, one of Japan's largest water supply reservoirs, where construction had just begun. The water from this reservoir is used to generate electricity at the Tama River Power Station directly below, and then discharged into the Tama River, where it passes through two water screens or filters to become the source of the nation's capital city's water supply. The scenery of the Okutama Dam, with its surrounding mountains of fresh greenery, reminded Hatta of the scenery of the Chianan Plain, and for a while he was in a daze thinking of Taiwan.

Hatta spent a relaxing time in Tokyo, but also kept busy, walking around a lot. On May 3, he and his son-in-law, Fukao, had dinner together at the Imperial Hotel. After seeing him off, he wrote a letter to Toyoki and the children. He handed the letter to the hotel staff to post, walked to Tokyo Station, and headed for the ticket gate of the Tōkaidō Line, where he had agreed to meet up with his subordinates.

The overnight train departed at 8:40 p.m. and the four of them sat facing each other, talking about their respective experiences in Tokyo until they fell asleep in their seats. Dawn appeared when they were arriving at Kyoto Station the next morning, and later that day at 2:00 p.m. on the 4th, they arrived in Hiroshima. They proceeded to the branch office of the Ministry of Colonial Affairs where they were instructed to meet at the Ujina Port wharf at 10:00 a.m. on the following day, the 5th.

Hatta told the three men accompanying him that they would be free until the following morning and explained that once they started working in the Philippines, they would not be able to sleep for a couple of months. He proposed they go to an inn at Miyajima and have some drinks. He said the sashimi would be good there, as well. Hatta offered to treat them. No one disagreed with his suggestion to head over there right away.

They were given a room in the annex of the Iwaso Ryokan, a famous inn. It was the first time for Hatta as well as his companion to stay in such a nice room. The Otorii gate of Itsukushima Shrine stood behind the Momijidani Valley. Hatta was not much of a drinker, but he told himself that that day would be special, and the four of them drank two bottles of *sake* before falling asleep. At dawn, Hatta woke up and headed for Itsukushima Shrine, leaving the three still asleep.

As he walked through the vermilion-lacquered Shrine building, which was connected to the main shrine by a wooden gate, and looked up at the large torii gate, Hatta hummed the famous poem by Saigyō, a monk-poet who lived a thousand years before, "I don't know what is happening, but I'm in tears of shame."[3]

The four of them arrived at Ujina Wharf at 9:00 a.m. A large contingent of 1,360 people, including 1,010 engineers, 34 military personnel, and crew members, who had been designated as personnel to be dispatched for development in the southern areas, was organized here. They consisted of civilians in national uniforms (a type of clothing developed for men in 1940) and suits, and military personnel in uniform.

The ship was the 16,000-ton *Taiyō Maru* of the NYK Line. The ship was more than thirty years old, but it was a huge ship with six floors of rooms. It could carry 1,360 passengers. Hatta told his three subordinates that they were going on a good ship. Although the ship had been in service for a long time, it had undergone several refurbishments during that time and seemed to be well equipped. The cabin was also satisfactory, as one would expect from a luxury cruise ship, even if old.

One by one, the personnel boarded the small barges that were traveling between the harbor wharf and the *Taiyō Maru* anchored offshore. After climbing up the ladder that had been lowered from the ship, Hatta, Miyaji, and Yumoto entered the cabin of the ship, which was quite nice and seemed to be used by senior officers. Ichikawa was not allowed to share the room, probably because of his junior position as a technician, and another room was assigned to him. He came to Hatta's cabin to tell him he was going to be in a different room. That was the last time Hatta saw him.

The ship departed from Moji, in Kitakyushu, around 3:00 p.m. on May 7, headed west along the Hibikinada Sea without incident, and dropped anchor at Mutsurejima, a lava plateau northwest of Hikoshima.

THE TRAGEDY OF THE *TAIYŌ MARU*

Taiyō Maru was not the only ship traveling at this time.[4] The fleet consisted of five vessels: the *Mikage Maru* of the NYK Line, which linked Shanghai and Kobe; the *Yoshino Maru* of the Kinkai Line, which operated the Taiwan route; and the *Shinyō Maru*, *Dōbaa Maru*, and *Taiyō Maru*. The *Taiyō Maru* was the ship that carried Japan's most valuable group of more than 100 engineers who were dispatched to develop the southern areas. There should have been two or three layers of maritime escort, but perhaps there was already a shortage of ships, so three ships, the *Peking Maru* belonging to the 1st Maritime Escort Force, the destroyer *Minekaze* belonging to the Sasebo Guard District, and the special gunboat *Futtsu Maru*, were assigned to escort the group from Mutsurejima to Taiwan. By 5:00 p.m. on May 8, the *Minekaze* and the *Futtsu Maru* had, for reasons uncertain, returned to Sasebo.

The slow-moving flotilla turned westward and passed the Gotō Islands, the westernmost island of Kyushu. At around 6:50 p.m. on the same day, tragedy struck the *Taiyō Maru*.

At 6:30 p.m. a banquet was held in the *Taiyō Maru*'s mess hall to celebrate the fall of Corregidor, with Hatta, Miyaji, and Yumoto all in attendance.

Corregidor Island is located off the coast of the Bataan Peninsula in the Philippines and was a key military point for the U.S. military. On the night of May 5, Japan launched a landing operation and secured a bridgehead under heavy fire from U.S. forces. Eventually, the defenders on Corregidor Island fell to the Japanese. In the Pacific War, the invasion of the Philippines by Japanese forces was one of the fiercest battles, and the fight for Corregidor was its climax. When news of the fall of Corregidor reached Japan, the whole country was excited. Although only red celebratory rice and a cup of sake were handed out, the celebrations on the *Taiyō Maru* were quite lively.

At this time, the U.S. military was busy producing large numbers of torpedoes, aiming to destroy the Japanese Navy, troop carriers, and supply ships with submarine-mounted torpedoes. Fifty-six submarines were deployed in the Pacific Ocean, leaving Pearl Harbor, Hawaii, in search of large Japanese

Figure 5.4   The Taiyō Maru at Sea. *Source*: (courtesy of NYK Line)

ships. One of the submarines, the USS *Grenadier*, spotted a fleet of ships moving slowly southward past the Danjo Islands, belonging to Nagasaki Prefecture, 70 kilometers southwest of the Gotō Islands. It set its sights on the *Taiyō Maru*, which was in front, and with the ship still visible at sunset, fired four torpedoes at it.

In the midst of this celebration, the ship was struck by what sounded like a lightning strike and felt like being smashed by a huge rock. The torpedo had hit the starboard stern. The buzz in the mess hall died down for a moment. Someone in the group next to Hatta said in a frightened tone that it felt like they had been hit by a torpedo. Others in the room began to shout "Torpedoes! Torpedoes!" Hatta urged Miyaji and Yumoto to go back to their room to put on their life vests. Hatta's decision was swift.

Putting on their life vests, the three men left the room. As they ran up the first four or five flights of stairs to the deck, a group of enlisted men who were returning to their quarters came screaming down the stairs. The three of them were pushed aside by the group.

When they finally made it to the upper deck, they discovered that the second torpedo had struck the starboard side and ripped through the ship. Flames were already erupting on the starboard stern where the first shot had hit. It was only a matter of time before the entire ship would be engulfed in flames. Nearly all the crew had put their life vests on and gathered tightly on the deck. One of the senior officers yelled out that the enemy had started its attack and that it was unsafe to be on the deck. He told everyone to return to their cabins.

The crew went back to their quarters. Miyaji hid himself in a small space at the doorway of the deck to avoid being swallowed by the waves of people. In that short time, Hatta and Yumoto were nowhere to be seen.

Miyaji was finally able to move himself and staggered out onto the upper deck again to reach the deck fence. Several escape lifeboats were being lowered into the water with ropes attached to each end. Miyaji approached one of them. Get in quickly, he was told.

Miyaji jumped onto the stern of the boat, which held about forty people, and got down low. At the same time, one of the ropes on the stern side of the boat snapped with a dull thud. The lifeboat was forced to hang vertically, and all the occupants were thrown out. In the process of falling, Miyaji's hat and glasses were blown off into the sea below.

THE DISCOVERY OF THE BODIES

The water was dark.[5] As Miyaji fell through the air, he clearly remembered the moment the blue-black sea closed in on him. He entered the water, but the buoyancy of his life vest propelled him back up, and he looked around. There was no sign of the forty or so people who had fallen from his lifeboat. He could see the next lifeboat in the water, and he swam with all his strength to catch it. He was still wearing his clothes and shoes, but surprisingly, he made progress.

Thanks to his life vest, he was able to swim for about twenty or thirty minutes before reaching the lifeboats. The sea had turned jet black. He put his hand on the edge of the boat, but there was no one to pull him up. Those in the boat were trying to escape the big whirlpool being created by the sinking *Taiyō Maru*. Someone, paddling frantically, told him to hold on and wait. Miyaji tried to raise himself up but couldn't, even using both hands. He tried next to swing his leg up but was unsuccessful.

He waited for a big wave to hit, thinking it would lift him up. When it did, he jumped up with the wave, heaved himself up to his chest, gathered all his remaining strength, and tumbled into the boat. Catching his breath, he looked ahead to see that the bow of the *Taiyō Maru* had turned upright and was disappearing into the sea with uncanny speed.

Miyaji had an ominous premonition that Hatta, Yumoto, and Ichikawa might still be inside the sinking ship. The spray of the waves hitting the lifeboat made the Noctiluca emit a pale blue light, which then disappeared. This made Miyaji all the more worried and scared.

During the night, the leader of the lifeboat had them take turns manning the oars. The lifeboat gradually made its way in the direction of the Gotō Islands. Helping too, Miyaji did not get a moments rest.

Around 10:00 a.m. on the 9th, the *Minekaze* and *Futtsu Maru*, both of which had left to return to Sasebo shortly after departing Mutsurejima, returned to help with the rescue operations for the *Taiyō Maru*. The ships lowered a series of rope ladders and ropes, and the displaced passengers and crews raced to cling to them, twisting and turning as they climbed aboard. Miyaji made a loop at the end of the rope and stuck one foot in it to pull himself up.

He finally reached the deck and sat down. He came to his senses realizing he had indeed survived when he popped a shot glass of whiskey into his mouth that had been given to him.

On May 10, both the survivors and the bodies of those that had died were returned to Nagasaki aboard the *Minekaze* and the *Futtsu Maru*. The survivors were taken to inns in Nagasaki, and the injured were taken to a nearby army hospital.

Miyaji was kept at an unknown inn, but he was so worried about Hatta, Yumoto, and Ichikawa that he could not stay there. He tried to get information from the officer in charge, but he was told bluntly that the incident was a military secret and that he could not talk about the specifics now.

After a couple of days, the survivors, who were lying in a state of numbness, were given a summary of the incident on the condition that they would not divulge any information to the outside world. Of the five ships in the fleet, only the *Taiyō Maru* had been sunk. Five-hundred forty-three survivors had been rescued, while the number of fatalities reached 817. Miyaji persisted in asking those concerned about the fate of Hatta, Yumoto, and Ichikawa, saying that since it was the governor-general's office that had sent them, it must be informed. However, he was not given an answer.

Nevertheless, the governor-general's office in Taiwan received a report of the three deaths on May 17 from the military. The technician, Shirakihara Tamiji, who had traveled with Hatta to the United States to purchase materials and equipment for the construction of the Chianan Irrigation System, had been sent to the Tokyo office to investigate the situation.

The news of the discovery of Hatta's body, later, was unexpectedly relayed to the Tokyo office through the Hagi City municipal government in Yamaguchi Prefecture. It was June 10th. Andō Akira, a fisherman from Hagi and captain of the *Dai 2 Riku Maru*, spotted a dark shadow drifting in the sea near Mishima. He approached it and pulled it out of the water, not thinking it was a body. Although it was still clothed, the flesh was gone and only a skeleton remained. He stopped fishing and took the body to the Hagi City Office. The person in charge at the city hall had no idea what Hatta looked like, but he found a business card in the victim's pocket identifying him as "Hatta Yoichi, Imperial Engineer of the Taiwan Governor-General's Office." The official immediately contacted the Tokyo office.

The Tokyo office informed his eldest son, Akio, what had happened. Akio could not believe it. He had just recently seen his father, if even for a short time at dinner, before his departure for the Philippines. He thought of his father's strong figure, who did not look old at all.

However, facts are facts. As the eldest son, he decided that he had to confirm it with his own eyes first and hurried to Hagi with Shirakihara.

Looking out the window of the train on the San'in Line at the black waters of the Sea of Japan, Akio felt empty. When he saw his father lying in a coffin at a temple in Hagi, Akio was able to confirm at a glance that it was his father from his clothes and skeletal shape, although his bones had since turned white. Hatta had been drifting in the sea for more than a month since the sinking of the *Taiyō Maru* and his flesh had been completely scraped off, leaving him a strange and eerie appearance of nothing more than "clothed" white bones. He was cremated at the temple. There was a small, private funeral service attended by Akio, Shirakihara, and a city hall official.

Akio wondered if he should take his father's remains to the family temple in Kanazawa, or take them to Taiwan where his mother, Toyoki, siblings, and everyone involved in the development of the Chianan Plain were waiting. Akio thought his father would probably want to be taken to Taiwan. He checked with Shirakihara, who agreed, that would probably have been Hatta's wishes.

After Hatta's remains were laid to rest for a while at his home in Taipei's Saiwai-chō, three memorial services were held in July. The first was held by the Hatta family at the Taipei branch of the Shinshū Ōtani sect, known as Higashi Honganji Temple in Kotobuki-chō. The second one was held in the middle of the month by the governor-general's office. The final one was held by those connected to the Chianan Irrigation System project in front of the statue of Hatta built near the dam at Wushantou in his honor shortly after his death.

FIVE POSTCARDS ADDRESSED TO THE CHILDREN

Hatta had sent a letter to Toyoki dated May 3, 1942, just before he left Tokyo for the Philippines. He was about to have dinner with his son-in-law, Fukao Tatsuo, at the Imperial Hotel before meeting up with his three subordinates who would accompany him to the Philippines via Hiroshima. While he was waiting for Fukao, he took out stationery and postcards from his bag and wrote.

Akio had to go to university early in the morning and as soon as he returned home, he had to practice rowing, so he could not go out until seven o'clock and could not have dinner with us. I told him to come to the Imperial Hotel at 6 p.m. because we were leaving tonight, but he said he could not come. Masako is unable to come as well because of the baby, so I will dine with Tatsuo only. After eating at the hotel, I will take the 8:40 p.m. third-class express train to Hiroshima, arriving at 2 p.m. tomorrow. I will report to the Ministry of Colonial Affairs, and at 9:00 a.m. on the 5th, I will report to the Transportation Department at XX. It will apparently take eight days to get to Manila. We may stop in Keelung or Kaohsiung, but we don't know. If we stop in Keelung, I will go to Taipei. If we stop in Kaohsiung, I will send a telegram to you and have you come there.[6]

Hatta had to self-censor part of the letter about departing from Ujina, as they were warned about providing too much information, even to one's spouse.

Hatta had been on many long overseas trips and been away from home for long periods in Taiwan and Japan, without complaining. Toyoki wondered why he was complaining about Akio and Masako not having come to see him off this one time, and why she was writing about how she wanted to meet them in Taipei or Kaohsiung, even if it was just for a short time. She thought his letter strange.

In addition to that, on the same day, there was another delivery of postcards addressed to the children. He had never written to them before. As she looked at the five postcards, she again felt that something strange was happening. It would be an exaggeration to call it an ominous premonition, but the children also wondered why their father had written. Toyoki told them she would save the postcard in a bureau drawer, as it was the first time for them. The children seemed unconcerned, and Toyoki thought better of it and calmed himself down, saying to herself that there was nothing to it.

On June 13, the governor-general's office informed the Wushantou Sub-branch Office of the *Taiyō Maru*'s sinking. A person from the office hurried to Toyoki with the news of the sinking. She asked what happened to her husband. He explained that the governor-general's office had not yet been informed of the names of the missing people, and that he would contact her as soon as they found out. He asked her to wait a little longer. Feeling embarrassed, he straightened himself up and left as quickly as he came.

Toyoki began to think that the letter and postcards had been an omen. It was not like her husband to say that he wanted to meet in Keelung or Kaohsiung, nor was it like him to write letters of encouragement to his children.

She reread the letter and the postcards to the children that she was keeping in the drawer. She waited impatiently for news, but nothing came. She went through the motions of housework but felt empty. She could not bring herself to eat anything. She decided not to mention it to her children until she knew for sure what had happened, so as not to upset them. Hiroko, Reiko, and Shigeko talked quietly among themselves but kept their mouths shut in front of their mother, uncomfortable with her unusual appearance.

Four days later, on June 17th, the staff member of the Sub-branch Office brought a document stating that Hatta had died in the line of duty along with Yumoto and Ichikawa. He explained that the head of the office would be coming shortly to pay his respects and departed. Toyoki was in shock. She collapsed on a table, pounding it in frustration and crying.

TOYOKI'S LAST DAYS, EVACUATED TO WUSHANTOU

Taiwan, the key point for the Japanese army's deployment south, would certainly become a target for the U.S. military.[7] The 10th Army, led by the last governor-general of Taiwan, General Andō Rikichi, was stationed in Taipei.

On October 12, 1944, Taipei was bombed by U.S. forces for the first time, but not much damage was done. People were frightened by the ominous feeling that a large-scale air raid would eventually come. On May 31, 1945, Taipei was attacked indiscriminately by U.S. bombers, killing about 300 people, and Hsinchu, Kaohsiung, and Tainan were also bombed.

Even while living in Taipei's Saiwai-chō and waiting for Hatta's return, Toyoki had begun to think that they needed to evacuate to the suburbs somewhere. The only place that came to mind was to go to Wushantou. It was the only place where the family could live together. It had been fifteen years since they had moved from Wushantou back to Taipei. During that time, she had been busy raising their eight children, and they were all growing up well. She was now forty-five years old.

The eldest daughter, Masako, married into the Fukao family in Tokyo and was the mother of two children. The fourth daughter, Yoshiko, was living with Masako while attending a girls' school in Tokyo. The eldest son, Akio, graduated from Tokyo Imperial University, volunteered for the Navy, and was currently serving in the Sasebo Naval District. The second son, Yasuo, was currently enrolled in Taipei High School, and stayed behind. Toyoki left Taipei with her remaining daughters, Hiroko (the third daughter), Reiko (the fifth daughter), and Shigeko (the youngest) and set up a female household in Wushantou.

It was the first time in a long while to live in the staff quarters. Most of the children had been born in that house in Wushantou as Hatta continued to work tirelessly. The staff quarters looked exactly the same as it had when they had left there for Taipei a decade and a half before.

It was sort of a homecoming for Toyoki. While the number of people she knew had declined, there were many familiar faces there. Akabori Shinichi, one of Hatta's former subordinates, was living in the staff quarters next door with his wife and four children. This was reassuring to her.

It was in April 1945, just before the end of the war, when Toyoki and her girls evacuated to Wushantou. U.S. forces were attacking the mainland and the Pacific War was raging in Japan and Okinawa.

On August 15, 1945, Akabori informed her that Japan had accepted the Potsdam Declaration and surrendered. His face was pale and drawn, as if something were imminent, though his expression was usually calm. On August 31, Yasuo, who had been mobilized as a student, was released from mobilization at the end of the war and headed to Wushantou. Hiroko happened to be in Taipei for something and was away then.

Toyoki, Yasuo, Reiko, and Shigeko had dinner together. Yasuo was curious as to why his mother, who usually asked him about his recent activities, was so quiet that night, but he did not feel anything especially odd about it. When he first moved to Wushantou, Yasuo faintly remembered his sister telling him, as they walked over the dam, that their mother had said if Japan lost the war, she wanted to jump in and die there. But he interpreted that to mean his mother thought that there was no way that Japan would lose.

Still, as he crawled under the covers, he felt that his mother had acted strange that night. At first, he could not sleep, but eventually he fell asleep.

After making sure that the children had gone to bed, Toyoki sat down at her husband's desk, acknowledging some letters, and then laid down.

She felt as if her body was no longer her own, and that she was lighter than ever. It was as if her soul had slipped out of her body and her opaque self had wandered out onto the dam. The next day would be September 1, the twenty-fifth anniversary of the start of construction for the Chianan Irrigation System.

She had married Hatta at the age of sixteen and had spent most of her life serving her husband, who had completed that great project. Her children had all started their own paths. She was still worried about the little one but was sure Akio or Masako and the others would take care of her.

It may have been an illusion, but it was very clear. She believed she heard her husband's voice. She got out of bed and changed into her formal clothes with the family crest on it.

As she walked out the front door of their house, she put on her white *tabi* (socks), *mompe* (loose trousers tied at the ankles), and new sandals, and pointed her feet toward the outlet of the Wushantou Dam.

It was raining heavily but she did not hear the rain. Soaking wet, she walked to the outlet. She placed her sandals on the concrete next to the spillway, put her hands together, threw herself into the spillway, which was now flooded with rain, and then disappeared.

A staff member who came to manage the spillway on the early shift found the sandals arranged neatly and called the villagers to see if they could find her. All hands went out to look for Toyoki, but they were unsuccessful. The previous day's heavy rain had made the spillway muddy, and the water level had risen. Despite repeated searches, her body was still not found by September 2. They searched not only at the mouth of the spillway but also downstream along the spillway, but could not find her body.

On September 3, after closing the valve of the spillway and searching the entire channel from upstream to down below, they found her body 6 kilometers downstream. As there was no crematorium at Wushantou, she was cremated by making a fire with branches in the area.

In a corner of the Wushantou Dam, there is a bronze statue that those involved with the project made for Hatta before he left Wushantou. Toyoki now rests with Hatta under a small granite tomb built behind the statue.

NOTES

1. Taihoku Beikoku Jimusho, ed., *Kanan Taishū: Beikoku Jimusho Chōsa* (Chianan Irrigation: Office of Rice and Wheat Study), 1936, located in Kōeki Zaidan Hōjin Doboku Gakkai Doboku Jinbutsu Aakaibusu Hatta Yoichi Kanren Shiryō (Hatta Yoichi Related Materials in the Archives of People of the Japan Society of Civil Engineers).

2. Kōkyō Hishū Kanan Taishū Kumiai, *Kōkyō Hishū Kanan Taishū Shinsetu Jigyō Gaiyō*.

3. Saigyō, *Saigyō Hōshi Kashū* (Collection of Poetry of Saigyō the Monk).

4. See Miyachi Suehiko, "Sōnan no Ki (A Record of the Disaster at Sea)," Hokkoku Shimbunsha Shuppankyoku, ed., *Kaisō no Hatta Yoichi*.

5. See Hatta Gishi Fusai o Shitai Taiwan to Yūkō no Kai, ed., *Mizu Akari: Hatta Yoichi Zuishiroku* (Faint Reflection of Light on Water in the Dark: Various Memories of Hatta Yoichi), (Kanazawa: Hokkoku Shimbunsha, 2020). This book is a re-issue of one privately published by Hatta's wife in 1943.

6. Ibid.

7. See Kai Jun, *Hatta Yoichi no Tsuma: Taiwan ni Tōyōichi no Damu o Tsukutta Hatta Gishi no Tsuma* (Hatta Yoichi's Wife: The Wife of the Engineer Who Made the Greatest Dam in the Orient) (Tokyo: Tsuge Shobō, 2017).

Chapter 6

Reason, Boldness, and the Administrative Style of Kodama and Gotō

KODAMA'S INTUITION IN APPOINTING GOTŌ AS GOVERNOR-GENERAL

The Sino-Japanese War ended in victory for Japan. On April 17, 1895, the two countries concluded the Treaty of Shimonoseki, and Taiwan came under Japanese control.

In the early years of Japanese rule, it was the problem of the "local bandits" that really bothered administrators. These were, as discussed in chapter 3, indigenous gangs who plundered and assaulted. There were mostly groups of revelers, thieves, and vigilantes. They varied in character, but they were a major factor in making the early years of Japan's administration of Taiwan extremely difficult.

Diplomatic documents show that just prior to the exchange of ratification papers for the peace treaty, Li Hong-zhang, the Qing plenipotentiary in the Sino-Japanese negotiations, sent a telegram to Itō Hirobumi, the Japanese plenipotentiary, that said:

> There has been a violent disturbance among the various peoples of Taiwan, and I have therefore been entrusted by His Majesty the Emperor with the task of readjusting the draft of the treaty with regard to the possession of Taiwan, after due consideration and reconsideration on the part of Japan. For this purpose, I sincerely hope that I can obtain the friendly cooperation of Minister Itō.[1]

During the Sino-Japanese peace talks, Li also insisted that Japan's control of Taiwan would indeed not be an easy task, telling Itō during their talks that

I have received a telegram from the governor of Taiwan saying that there is already a rumor circulating in Taiwan that the island is to be ceded to Japan, and that the people are very much agitated. This is what he said. The reason I am telling your Excellency this now is not to sway your will regarding your demands for Taiwan, but only to contribute in a friendly manner to your Excellency's understanding of the situation.[2]

Although the peace treaty was concluded at Shimonoseki and the cession of Taiwan was stipulated in the treaty, as Li had prophesized, Japan's rule over Taiwan did not begin in a stable manner at this time. This was because the people of Taiwan did not cooperate in Japan's control of Taiwan. On the contrary, they were extremely defiant. Japan had to use its military power to "conquer" Taiwan, which had already been ceded by the treaty.

Japan decided that the occupation of Taiwan should be completed in a hurry and deployed a large number of troops. In May 1895, the Japanese army made General Kabayama Sukenori the first governor-general of Taiwan, and together with the Imperial Guards Division under the command of Prince Kitashirakawa Yoshihisa, they landed in Tamotsu, occupied Keelung, and entered Taipei without bloodshed. The next step was the capture of Tamsui, and the northern part of Taiwan swiftly fell into Japanese hands.

As the Japanese troops headed south, they met fierce resistance by the Taiwanese people. In response, Japan deployed the 2nd Division under the command of Lieutenant General Nogi Maresuke. The total number of Japanese troops involved in the occupation of Taiwan was approximately 50,000 in two army divisions, 26,000 military dependents, and 9,500 war horses. This was more than one-third of the army's strength at the time, and most of the Allied Fleet. It was the "other Sino-Japanese War."[3]

During the three years of the first three governors-general, Kabayama, Katsura Tarō, and Nogi, the greatest challenge was how to suppress the resistance of the local bandits. The governor-general devoted all his energies to defeating the local bandits by force, but without success, the defeats often had the opposite effect of fanning the flames of resistance of the local bandits. Defeating the rebels led to massacres, and those who were related to the victims ended up joining the rebels, with the rebellion showing no signs of abating.

As the cost of defeating the rebels increased, the amount of money spent by Japan to replenish the shortage of troops also rose steadily. The management of Taiwan ended up only increasing the financial burden on the home government, and in the Imperial Diet in 1897, the sale of Taiwan to France was even discussed.

With the arrival of Kodama Gentarō as the fourth governor-general, Taiwan's governing policy entered a period of major change. Kodama had a rich conceptual ability and was able to quickly turn his ideas into policies. Moreover, he selected the best people to carry out his policies. In the modern history of Japan, there are not many leaders with such diverse talents and strong spirit. If Kodama had not been appointed governor-general in the early years of the administration, the modernization of Taiwan might have ended in a disastrous failure. Kodama, a military strategist known to all, was an exceptional statesman who fully demonstrated the authority and power he had acquired through military politics in governing Taiwan.[4]

One of Kodama's major achievements was his selection of Gotō Shinpei, a skilled bureaucrat, as the governor-general office's director for Civil Affairs and his bringing him to Taiwan. This process can be seen in the actions of the two men: Gotō's idea of governance, which is discussed later, was "embodied" in Kodama, and that idea of governance was further refined on the ground in Taiwan. As Kodama trusted the men he selected, Gotō had great power to implement the policies he felt best to pursue.

It was when Kodama was vice minister of the army that he first came to know Gotō. Kodama was highly impressed by Gotō's skill in the medical quarantine of Japanese troops returning from victory in the Sino-Japanese War. They had to do everything they could to stop the cholera, typhoid, dysentery, and other infectious diseases brought by the repatriated soldiers from infecting the general public before they returned home.

Figure 6.1   Kodama Gentarō. *Source:* (courtesy of Gotō Shinpei Kinenkan)

Figure 6.2 Gotō Shinpei. *Source*: (courtesy of Gotō Shinpei Kinenkan)

There were 227 ships carrying the returning soldiers and more than 230,000 soldiers. Kodama was the vice minister of the army in charge of the quarantine.

It is often thought that war means fighting between opposing forces on the battlefield, with the respective generals commanding them. Of course, this is true, but war also has two extremely important administrative tasks: the maintenance of the troops' logistics in support of the war in the rear and the quarantine of returning soldiers. Without a statesman who possesses both military acumen and administrative skill, victory in a total war is not possible. At this time, Kodama was the military leader to do so.

It takes a tremendous amount of energy to keep more than 230,000 triumphant soldiers, who want to return to their hometowns as soon as possible with the excitement of victory in their hearts, at the quarantine station for a certain period of time. Kodama looked in all directions to see if there was anyone who had the administrative capability to utilize the medical techniques of quarantining and to do so efficiently.

Kodama's instincts told him that Gotō would be able to take care of the almost quarter-million soldiers who had returned to Japan. Gotō had been ousted from his position as the director general of the Health Bureau of the Home Ministry over an incident in which he was imprisoned for five months but later found innocent. He had had enough of being a government official and turned down Kodama's request.

However, he was overwhelmed by Kodama's hidden power and ability, which he had never seen before, and eventually decided to accept the offer. Interestingly, Gotō was from Mizusawa, a branch of the Sendai domain, which was a former rival of the Satsuma and Chōshū domains, which the Meiji government was centered on. With Kodama's full support, he was given the opportunity to display his talent, despite himself not having his own political base within the government.

The army would bear all the costs of quarantine. Gotō was free to plan the quarantine as he liked, but the deadline for the quarantine was three months from July 1, 1895. A temporary army quarantine department was set up with Kodama as its director, and Gotō became its de facto head. In this way, the major project that would set the direction of Gotō's life was launched.

Three islands were selected: Ninoshima Island off the coast of Ujina, Hiroshima Prefecture; Hikoshima Island at the southern tip of Shimonoseki; and Sakurajima facing Osaka Bay. Approximately 5,000 to 6,000 people were quarantined per day on Ninoshima Island, and 2,500 to 3,000 on Hikoshima and Sakurajima, respectively. This was the first quarantine project of this scale not only in Japan but also in the world.

Figure 6.3   Ninoshima Quarantine Area. *Source*: (courtesy of Gotō Shinpei Kinenkan)

After attending the Sukagawa Medical School in Fukushima Prefecture, interning at the Aichi Prefectural Hospital, and studying at the Robert Koch Institute in Germany, Gotō served as director general of the Health Bureau of the Home Ministry. During the quarantining, his skills were put to the test. Kodama gave him the opportunity to show off his talent. It was Kodama's influence that suppressed the outburst of complaints and dissatisfaction that swirled among the soldiers who were prevented from returning home by quarantine.

With the technical guidance of Kitasato Shibasaburō, a close friend of Gotō's who had lived with him in Germany, they installed the latest steam disinfectors and set up a strict, efficient, and effective quarantine system, completing the quarantine on schedule, within three months. Those who were found to have been stricken by disease or other illness were given the proper care and returned to their hometowns.

The number of soldiers suffering from real cholera, pseudo-cholera, typhoid fever, and dysentery was recorded as 369, 311, 126, and 179 men, respectively. If patients of this scale had been scattered across the country without the quarantine, the situation would have been quite serious. With his extensive medical training, Gotō believed that prevention was more important than simply trying to cure the disease.

"MY POLICY IS 'NO POLICY'"

As a result, Gotō was reinstated as director general of the Health Bureau of the Home Ministry, and then accompanied Kodama to Taiwan who had been appointed to serve as governor-general of Taiwan on February 26, 1898.[5] Gotō was appointed director of the Civil Affairs Bureau (later to become director general) on March 2, 1898, when Kodama was forty-six years old and Gotō was forty-one.

After assuming the post of governor-general of Taiwan, Kodama, accompanied by Gotō, made frequent inspections, mainly in areas where there were a lot of local bandits. With few words, he simply observed the scene. Kodama was deeply troubled by the situation in Taiwan, where the local bandits were rampant.

Since he had been assigned as governor-general of Taiwan, he was expected to issue instructions regarding his policies at the time of his inaugural address, as Kabayama, Katsura, and Nogi had done so as well.

He called Gotō and ordered him to draft an instruction. However, Gotō said something surprising—that the policy should be one of "no policy." It was important, he argued, to consider the habits and customs that existed in Taiwan from old and to adopt policies that fit these customs rather than simply superimposing their views and policies on the island. He explained that it was biologically impossible to simply transplant organisms grown in one region to another region. They had to adapt.

This was the "principle of biology," a theory long held by Gotō. He believed Kodama would understand his thinking and wanted to impress upon him this idea at the outset. It was a unique opportunity to convey his ideas to Kodama and instill them in his mind. He said,

> Your Excellency, the policy of Taiwan's administration must be based on the fundamentals of biology. If we are to build Taiwan's administration on the basis of biology, we must respect the customs and habits that have been handed down from generation to generation in Taiwan. However, this does not mean that we should be stuck with the old customs and make do with what we have. On the one hand, we should respect the old customs as much as possible, and on the other hand, we should make thorough improvements where necessary. If we do this, the resistance of the people will gradually decrease. Your Excellency, let's follow this policy at all costs. I will serve you with all my strength.[6]

Kodama's eyes suddenly seemed to sharpen. Gotō's intuition told him that Kodama had understood the core of the matter at once. Gotō continued,

> It is difficult to change the hearts and minds of officials and the Taiwanese people with a single message from His Excellency. In fact, it may be impossible to do so. There is no other way but to prove the correctness of Japan's rule with facts. I think we need time to do that.

Kodama's face showed a look of understanding on it. Kodama wondered if Gotō had finished his sermon, but Gotō's oratory continued:

> His Excellency has not come to dig up the soil of Taiwan. The most important duty of the governor-general is to establish the basis for the colonial policy of the Empire. In order to do so, His Excellency must use his firm plow to dig up the difficult problems in Taiwan that only you can do. I believe that His Excellency's most urgent task is to raise the awareness of the prime minister and other cabinet members and politicians.

Kodama did not ask any questions at this point, but simply said, "All right." Kodama's thoughts on Taiwanese policy seemed to have run their course. What had been in his mind for a long time was now verbalized and clarified by Gotō's "sermon." Gotō was solemnly impressed by Kodama's intuitive judgment. In the end, Kodama gave a formal greeting at the inauguration, but as an instruction, he said to the effect, "My policy is 'no policy'."

Kodama had committed himself to the view that the administration would prove itself by its performance.

During their respective reigns as governor-general, Kabayama, Katsura, and Nogi had to deal with the conquest of local bandits, which resulted in heavy financial expenditures and a large deficit in the budget. This deficit ultimately had to be covered from the Japanese government's general account, and Taiwan was perceived as a great burden for Japan. As mentioned earlier, there was even discussion of selling Taiwan in the Imperial Diet.

The battle against the local bandits was bloody. During the reigns of Kabayama and Katsura, all energy was devoted to pacification and nothing else could be done. Nogi's arrival as the third governor was charged with the task of suppressing the local rebels through a unique strategy called "three-tier security." Three-tiered security meant that the army and the military police would be deployed in mountainous and remote areas where the local bandits occupied complex areas, the civilian police would take care of the plains and urban areas, and the military police and the civilian police would work together to deal with the areas in between.

However, even with this method, the local bandits could not be easily defeated, and on the contrary, they ended up increasing in strength. The army, military police, and civilian police all had different chains of command, and the scene became confused, and sometimes they even clashed with each other. The weakness of the three-tier security system was that it was difficult to distinguish between the local bandits and the "good people." In peacetime, even the local rebels lived in harmony with the common people, and it was impossible to identify and subdue only the local rebels. The actions of overzealous Japanese soldiers frequently resulted in the injury and death of civilians, who became embittered, and which led to an increase in the power of the local bandits.

HOW TO DEAL WITH ARMED "BANDITS"

It was Gotō's turn to deal with the armed bandits. Gotō advised Kodama to take measures to invite the local bandits to surrender, which he did, and the surrender was quickly accomplished.[7] Rather than using military force to subdue the local rebels, this policy focused on the tradition of self-government that had taken root in each of Taiwan's settlements, and it was a "patrol policy," in the broad sense of the word, to convert the main force of the local rebels into good citizens through a self-government mechanism centered on the civilian police. The police in Taiwan, as conceived by Gotō, not only engaged in regular police activities but also in administrative services, such as tax collection, educational promotion for children, and even work as local judges, and was fostered as an organization closely connected to the lives of the people at the end of society.

Although the local bandits seemed to have been spread out in countless numbers, a detailed investigation revealed that there were three notable big bandits, including Lin Hwai-wang in Yilan in the east, Chen Qiu-ju and five others near Taipei in the north, He Tie and three others in the center, Zheng Jicheng and two others in the south, and about twenty others in total. Gotō believed that if they focused on the leaders and taught them the truth, the way would be opened for their rehabilitation and for peace.

If they were persuaded to return to good citizenship, the government would provide them with tax exemption, rehabilitation funds, and job opportunities in road and other construction. The smaller bandits began to return after learning that the more well-known bandits had ended their struggle.

After repeated persuasion, Yilan Governor Saigō Kikujirō hired the bandits who had returned to Yilan to work on the embankment construction, and succeeded in controlling the Yilan River, which regularly flooded. This work, known as the "Saigō Dike," is still remembered in Taiwan today.

On the one hand, Kodama had initiated the policy to invite the bandits to surrender, but for those who did not, the "Order for the Punishment of Bandits" was issued in November 1898. Between 1901 and 1902, 12,000 Taiwanese forces who continued the resistance were killed.

The military was given a great deal of power in suppressing the banditry. The military had a strong sense of pride that it was the military who had brought about victory in the Sino-Japanese War and occupied Taiwan. As such, the military was greatly dissatisfied with Kodama and Gotō's policy of inviting the rebels to surrender and patrolling them. A standoff between military and administrative officials was inevitable. In order for the policy of inviting local rebels to surrender to be successful, it was necessary to overcome the dissatisfaction in the military.

Gotō, who had been assigned as the director of the Civil Affairs Bureau of the governor-general's office, invited the chief of the army staff, the Taipei brigade commander, the Taichung brigade commander, the Tainan brigade commander, and other key members of the military to the Seiryōkan, a restaurant overlooking the Tamsui River, in order to greet the military on his arrival.

Gotō had to arrive late for the banquet, which he had organized himself, due to unavoidable official duties. As Gotō took his seat, apologizing for his tardiness, the Taichung brigade commander, Matsumura Kanemoto, made a sarcastic remark to the effect that the host of the banquet should not be late.

Gotō, who had long been annoyed by the behavior of soldiers, whom he found arrogant and dismissive of civilians, replied in an equally sarcastic manner. Matsumura then criticized civil servants and boasted about his military prowess. Gotō stood in front of Matsumura, who already was tipsy, and said that military commanders simply stand behind their troops and give orders, letting others die. He then asked him had he ever suffered before, such as being unfairly arrested and sent to prison?

Gotō then hit Matsumura on the head and left. When he got home, he reflected on what happened. He was full of remorse, but there was no way to take it back.

The next morning, he called on Kodama, who was up early, in the garden of the governor-general's residence, and told him about the incident the night before. Kodama said very little.

That evening, Kodama had the military leadership gather at the governor-general's office and told them to the effect that there could not be any friction or fighting with the civilian side. He explained that he entrusted the civil administration to Gotō as director general and would take full responsibility for his actions. If the military had any problems, they should come directly to Kodama to talk about. Hearing Kodama's unshakable trust in Gotō, and witnessing his dignity, the assembled soldiers were made to straighten up once again, and from then on, their opposition to Gotō faded away, and the plan to invite the bandits to surrender began to take shape.

On May 25, 1898, Kodama gave the following instructions as the governor-general:

> There are two types of organizations that are prepared to deal with calamities: the civilian police and the military police. According to what I have heard, the military police are superior to the civilian police. From observation of actual conditions, it is clear that the regular police are better suited for civil affairs. In particular, it is unclear why there must still be a three-tiered police force. It is said that regarding the military's education the military police is superior, but the ability to prevent calamities before they occur and to make the best of those difficulties and turn them into good fortune are better suited for the civilian police if they can be utilized properly.[8]

In the "Instructions to the Chief of Staff of the Army and Navy and the Brigade Commanders" of June 3, 1898, Kodama stated: "My duty is to control Taiwan, not to conquer it." This was a very clear policy.

THE *HOKŌ* SYSTEM OF TAIWAN

When Taiwan was incorporated into the Qing Dynasty, a large number of people from Fujian and Guangdong provinces migrated to Taiwan.[9] There are also Malays and Polynesians who had lived in Taiwan for a long time before that. These latter groups were those who were driven from the plains to the mountains by migrants from Fujian and Guangdong. In the early days of the Japanese occupation, they were known as the "Seiban" and later as the "Takasago" tribes. The Seiban were difficult to suppress. While the focus of the Japanese administration was with fighting the local bandits, the Japanese and Han Chinese entered the traditional Seiban settlements in an uncontrolled manner, causing them to become an anti-Japanese force.

Although Japan introduced the same coercive policies against these rebels as it did against the local bandits, in the end, the final policy adopted here was the same as that against the local bandits—namely encouraging them to surrender. They succeeded in getting most of the island's residents to submit to the authority of the governor-general.

The ideas of Kodama and Gotō on governing Taiwan are well expressed in their efforts to reorganize and institutionalize the autonomous neighborhood organization known as "baojia," which had been handed down from generation to generation in Taiwan. It was through this neighborhood organization, renamed the *Hokō* system, that the local bandits were finally contained with the cooperation of the residents and local police. A *Hokō* ordinance was issued in August 1898.

Under this system, ten households were designated as one *kō*, and ten *kō* were designated as one *ho*, with a chief of each *kō* and *ho* being appointed. The respective groups would observe each other and be responsible for one another. Under this system, family registration, immigration control, prevention of contagious diseases, and construction of roads and bridges were carried out. Article 5 of the *Hokō* ordinance states that "the *Hokō* could appoint a group of young men to guard against banditry, water, and fire."

A "peace preservation corps" composed of able-bodied young men was formed as an auxiliary organization to the civilian police, and as a result, the bandits that had plagued Taiwan in the early years of its rule were almost completely eliminated. The *Hokō* system allowed the administration of Taiwan to reach all parts of the country.

In the early years of Taiwan's rule, Kodama and his colleagues were troubled by something else. This was the treatment of opium addicts. The number of opium smokers had reached 170,000 out of the estimated 3,000,000 residents of Taiwan at the time. A policy of "strict prohibition" would have driven the opium smokers into withdrawal and caused untold social confusion including deaths and crimes. However, if left unchecked, the addict problem would continue to spread, and Taiwan would not have been able to become a healthy, functioning society.

Gotō, a medical doctor by trade, adopted the "gradual ban" policy. He knew it was not possible to take all the opium away from the opium smokers at once. He issued the "Taiwan Opium Ordinance" and established a monopoly system for the sale of opium. The opium sales were limited to designated brokers and retailers, and only those who habitually smoked opium were allowed to purchase it. A "purchase book" was to be kept, and new smokers would not be issued a book. This was called the "Opium Smoking Patent Identification System."

The price of opium was set higher than in the past. As a result, the number of opium smokers decreased gradually, and the monopoly income increased. Although it took a long time because of the gradual ban, the number of opium smokers decreased from 170,000 in 1897 to slightly more than 60,000 by 1917. The monopoly system, the prototype of which was created in the opium policy, was later applied to salt, camphor, tobacco, and liquor.

Whether it was the suppression of local bandits or the gradual reduction of opium smokers, the success of these efforts was not in itself a development or modernization of Taiwan. However, without these accomplishments, the "initial conditions" for Taiwan's development and modernization could not have been created. These two tasks were perhaps even more difficult than the development and modernization themselves. Gotō, a rare political bureaucrat with a firm idea of governance (see below), was able to move Kodama to make this policy a reality.

Gotō was fond of saying that the colonial policy was "biology." Gotō's thinking on Taiwan's governance was already clearly expressed in the "An Emergency Proposal on the Governance of Taiwan" of 1898, which he drafted when he was still the director general of the Health Bureau in the Home Ministry.

> The basis of managing a colony must be entirely based on the principles of biology, fitting of today's advancements in science. What is the basis of biology? It is to promote scientific life, and to realize the foundations for production, industry, sanitation, education, transportation, police, etc., so that they can develop competitively and realize the principle of survival of the fittest. In the same way that animals can survive cold and heat, endure hunger and thirst, and adapt to their circumstances, we should be able to follow the times and places, overcome various difficulties, gain the approval of the authorities, and shine in the management of Taiwan.[10]

In essence, he was saying that this was the reason why they must formulate and enforce policies that would help the people of Taiwan.

Gotō's interest in Taiwan's old customs was astonishing. In 1941, the governor-general's office set up the "Provisional Research Council on the Old Customs of Taiwan" and assigned Okamatsu Santarō, a civil law scholar at Kyōto Imperial University, to investigate the legal system of land, kinship, inheritance, etc. in Taiwan. In addition, Akuzawa Naoya, who ran a rubber plantation in Malay, and bureaucrats from the Ministry of Finance and judges were invited to conduct field surveys on Taiwan's customs in agriculture, industry, commerce, and the economy.

"PRINCIPLES OF NATIONAL HYGIENE" AS THE BASIS FOR GOTŌ'S THINKING

There were many things that Kodama and Gotō had to do. They had no idea who was living where and under what conditions in Taiwan, the ethnicity of the people living in each area, and most importantly, the number of people living in each area. It would be impossible to govern Taiwan when the "initial conditions" themselves were uncertain. It was unclear how much land existed in Taiwan at the time Japan came into possession of the island. Both a land survey and a population survey were essential.

Kodama and Gotō arrived in Taiwan in March of 1898. The land survey project began in September of the same year. It was a huge undertaking. The Taiwan Land Survey Bureau was established in the governor-general's office, and over 800 people were mobilized and divided into dozens of teams, which worked in close cooperation with each other to survey the whole of Taiwan using the latest techniques and establish the land registry based on the survey.

A land registry survey is a survey to determine the owner, lot number, land classification, boundary, and area of each parcel of land. The land survey project was called one of the three major projects, along with the North-South Railway and the port construction projects for both Keelung in the north and Kaohsiung in the south.

The land system in Taiwan was extremely complicated, as a result of the fact that immigrants from Fujian, Guangdong, and other regions migrated to Taiwan at different times as clans, forcing the aborigines to move into the mountainous regions, while the clans competed with each other for land ownership.

These migrants from the mainland were the ones who took power in the process of driving the aborigines into the mountains. In the beginning, the powerful clans ruled through what were called "kenshou" (large landowners). The actual cultivators of the land were small landowners in the village, called "kenhu" who improved their productivity through the use of water and fertilizer to increase their power. Later, it became common for small farmers to be entrusted with the cultivation of the land. Looking at this as a land system, Taiwan's land was under a dual ownership system of large and small landowners. On the one hand, the small households paid a land fee called the "large rent" to the large householders, and, on the other hand, the smaller households rented out the land to tenant farmers and received "small rent."

There were different rights and obligations as well, making the system complex. It was necessary to create a uniform tax rate in order for the governor-general's office to properly tax the land for revenue purposes.

Surveys revealed the existence of a large number of unregistered plots with uncertain ownership known as "hidden fields." Gotō himself became the temporary director general of the Taiwan Land Survey Bureau, and the government's land survey project was carried out in a well-organized manner.

The head of the project was Nakamura Korekimi, who had been assigned as an administrative officer of the governor-general's office in 1896 and had been preparing for the land survey. Nakamura succeeded Gotō as director general of the Land Survey Bureau.

As a result of the discovery of the hidden fields, the total cultivated land area in Taiwan, which was estimated to be 360,000 hectares before the survey began, was actually determined to be 630,000 hectares, doubling the governor-general office's land tax revenue. The governor-general's office also undertook land reform by acquiring the rights of all large landowners and making small independent landowners. The land survey project contributed greatly to the expansion of the tax base, but it did not stop there. The survey included the entire landscape, topography, rivers, farmland, waterfalls, and so forth, and became an important source of information for the construction of the infrastructure that would later become the foundation for Taiwan's development as introduced in chapter 5.

After the completion of the land survey in 1905, a population census was conducted on the entire island simultaneously on the first day of October of the same year. Although a law to conduct a national census was passed by the Imperial Diet in 1902, the survey was not conducted. However, in Taiwan it was undertaken making Taiwan the first place for a population census to be done within the Empire in Japan's history. In addition to the population count, the census covered many other items, such as place of birth, sex, age, family, occupation, residence, language, opium-use, as well as the customs of foot-binding and queue hair (pigtail), and so forth, providing a numerical basis for the implementation of various policies in line with popular sentiment.

These projects originated from Gotō's beliefs as a civil administrator. In his thinking is found a firm conviction that was expressed in the "Principles of National Hygiene," which Gotō wrote in the midst of his extremely busy schedule in 1889, when he was thirty-three years old, while serving in the Bureau of Health.

Gotō approached Taiwan with a set of principles in mind as he took on the difficult political situation there in the early period of the administration during his more than eight years as director-general of Civil Affairs, leaving many noteworthy accomplishments. He possessed pre-determined principles

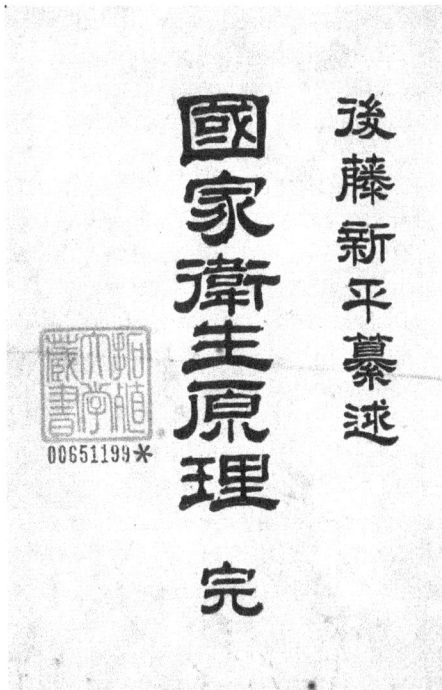

Figure 6.4   Cover of Original Version of Goto's *Principles of National Hygiene. Source*: (courtesy of Takushoku University)

and concepts when he went to Taiwan and managed to thoroughly achieve results, something quite unique in terms of "thought and reality."

In his "Principles of National Hygiene," the word "hygiene" as used by Gotō probably has a strong connotation of "preventative health," "public health," or even "communal welfare." As a physician and director general of the Bureau of Public Health previously in the Home Ministry, Gotō must have wanted to use improving health and hygiene as the symbol for good governance in Taiwan.

Gotō, who had a strong desire to promote public health in Taiwan, had been making several important proposals on public health policy, including opium policy, since the time he was public health director general of the Bureau of Public Health, even before he was assigned to Taiwan as director general of Civil Affairs. During his tenure as director general of the Bureau of Health, he was commissioned as the health advisor to the governor-general of Taiwan, and his recommendations had a considerable impact on the policies of the governor-general's office.

In June 1895, the governor-general's office established Taiwan Hospital, the first government-run medical clinic, in Taipei, and in the following year

(1896), the governor-general opened hospitals in Taichung and Tainan, gradually expanding the number of hospitals in major cities. In the same year, the governor-general's office invited doctors from the mainland of Japan and established a system of assigning a doctor to each area of Taiwan. Public physicians were stationed at the forefront of the fight against malaria and plague in Taiwan. In the thirtieth year of Meiji (1897), a medical school was established to train the children of Taiwanese residents as doctors. The Governor-General's Taipei Hospital later became the hospital attached to the Faculty of Medicine of the Imperial University of Taipei, and Gotō's "Principles of National Hygiene" was introduced to Taiwan as a standard for public health, which was realized there.

Charles Darwin was the biologist who explored the theory of the "Origin of the Species." Darwinism is based on the theory of evolution, which holds that the various organisms we see before us now have evolved over a long period of time to become what they are today. Darwinism is a theory that emerged in the nineteenth century and had a major influence on various sciences, leading to the widespread introduction of the concepts of "competition for survival" and "survival of the fittest." It also became a strong basis for what is known as Social Darwinism.

Social Darwinism is the basis for Gotō's biological principle, which he wrote about in his "Principles of National Hygiene":

> In the world of living things, competition for survival never ceases, not even for a moment, and we cannot deviate even a little from the principle of survival of the fittest. This idea is now unanimously accepted by all scholars. Therefore, all living things must resist the attack of competition, defend themselves against it, and properly feed themselves and reproduce in order to survive. There is no reason to think that humans are the exception to this rule.[11]

MASTER THE PRINCIPLE OF
SURVIVAL OF THE FITTEST

Gotō regarded human beings as those whose purpose in life is to achieve physiological harmony. Physiological harmony, or satisfaction, referred to "living conditions that are satisfactory for the sound development of the mind and body." The reason why human beings seek physiological harmony is because of the "physiological motivation" inherent in human beings. Gotō believed that ethics such as spiritualism, right and wrong, and good and evil do not dominate human beings, but that human beings weave their lives solely in search of physiological harmony.

Gotō believed that overcoming the competition for survival and surviving as the fittest is the "natural state" of human beings. However, if human beings can only survive in such a combative competition for survival, social order cannot be established. In a society of "struggle of all against all," it is difficult to expect the smooth formation of order. In order to establish social order, it is often necessary to create a "public force" with authority. The person who is tasked with enforcing public power is the "sovereign," in other words, the authority and power of the state. For the unification of society, "supreme authority" is necessary, and society cannot be established without submission to the supreme authority of the state.

In order for the competition for survival among individuals not to bring about the ruin of society, the supreme right as a sovereign power with reason is indispensable, and this is none other than the state or "nation" as referred to in the "Principles of National Hygiene." The creation of social order by the state is also physiologically motivated. The reason, Gotō wrote, is

> The organization of the state is derived from the physiological motivation of mankind, and its purpose is to satisfy the physiological needs of mankind. This would be the simplest and most accurate answer. It is for this reason that we seek national security and happiness, or to protect rights and order.[12]

To realize the survival of the fittest in the competition for survival is the only reason for the existence of the state, or power. It is this "biological principle" that must be realized on Taiwan's soil, Gotō insisted. The theory of social evolution and the way power is exercised based on this theory were the "bare bones" to Gotō.

However, and this was another important point in Gotō's thesis, state power should not be exercised unilaterally, ignoring the customs and institutions that have been handed down from generation to generation within individuals and groups. Rather, the customs and institutions of the "place" where the power was exercised should be fully respected and coordinated, and as much as possible not be in disagreement with these customs and institutions. This is where Gotō's thought process was refined.

One of the stories Gotō liked to cite was "The Flatfish's Eyes and the Sea Bream's Eyes." In the story, he would explain,

> Social conventions and institutions all arise for good reasons, out of longstanding necessity. Blindly attempting to impose the institutions of a civilized nation on a backward one, without understanding those reasons, is an act of tyranny by civilization. It mustn't be done.[13]

Gotō was a man who had a deep understanding of how to exercise power.

The strategy of inviting the local bandits to surrender, the land survey, and the investigation of old customs were all the result of Gotō's flexible and unconventional thinking, derived from the principle of "survival of the fittest." The reason why Gotō was able to realize these ideas in Taiwan was because Taiwan was a unique jurisdiction, different from mainland Japan.

Taiwan was not subject to Japan's constitution and various laws and was for the most part independent of the Imperial Diet. The argument for extending the same system as mainland Japan to Taiwan, known as the "internal extension principle," was not something that could be ignored, especially in the early years of the administration of the island, but in the end, Taiwan became its own jurisdiction separate from Japan through the "Law No. 63."

The main point of Law No. 63 was that "the Governor of Taiwan may issue orders having the force of law within the area under his jurisdiction." Taiwan was a jurisdiction governed by its own laws, called *ritsurei*, issued by the governor. Gotō's ideas were "embodied" in Kodama's policies, and with Kodama's authority, Gotō was able to freely spread his own governing ideas in Taiwan and to have officials and others he thought necessary for developing Taiwan.

A BANK OF TAIWAN AS NECESSARY FOR DEVELOPMENT

With the surrender of the bandits and the development of the tax collection base through the land survey project, the government was now ready to actively develop Taiwan, but in order to do so, it was essential to raise financial funds.[14] The defeat of the local bandits and the land survey project themselves were very costly, and the governor-general's budget deficit increased.

From the beginning, Gotō believed that unless the Bank of Taiwan were established, the bank underwritten, and Taiwanese government bonds issued on a large-scale using tax revenue as the source of redemption, it would not be possible to construct the North-South Railway up and down the western side of the island, build the ports of Keelung and Kaohsiung, or even carry out land survey projects. He wanted to make Taiwan independent of the Japanese government's finances, and he wanted to show the world powers that Japan was fully capable of managing overseas territories.

Six months after Gotō was transferred to Taiwan, he wrote a letter to Soeda Juichi, then vice minister of finance, who would later become the first president of the Bank of Taiwan. He told him,

Since the arrival of the present Governor-General, we have been reforming the administrative structure, redeploying the military, improving the discipline and morale of the bureaucracy, and preventing the spread of bandits. The management of the new territory has finally begun. At this time, in order to support the commercial and industrial enterprises and help them expand their business, it is necessary to have a financial institution that can respond to their needs, and it is regrettable that one has not yet been established. In view of this, I am eagerly awaiting the establishment of the Bank of Taiwan as soon as possible.[15]

The Bank of Taiwan was established in June 1899, and the "Taiwan Project Public Bond Act" was promulgated. By FY 1906, the bank had issued bonds fifteen times. Without the Bank of Taiwan, the development of Taiwan would not have been possible.

Both Kodama and Gotō shared the view that Taiwan should not become a financial burden for Japan and that Taiwan should achieve financial independence as soon as possible. In 1899, at the same time as the Bank of Taiwan was established, the governor-general's office announced the "Twenty-Year Fiscal Plan," which called for a gradual reduction in financial support from the home country, and for Taiwan to become financially independent from the year 1909 onward. It was an ambitious plan to issue public bonds for productive projects and to achieve a revenue surplus after deducting principal and interest from FY 1904 onward.

Figure 6.5   **Lobby of Bank of Taiwan.** *Source*: (courtesy of Sankei Shimbunsha)

Initially, the government was prepared to run a deficit, but it turned to a proactive approach to industrial promotion and encouraging the autonomous management of various projects as soon as possible to meet the principal and interest burden of the public debt. The plan included the construction of railroads and ports, government buildings, waterworks projects, reservoirs, the conducting of land surveys, and the development of forestry resources, such as at Alishan, all with the plan to end reliance on public bonds by 1909 and, in the case of national subsidies, by 1911.

Through the land survey project, otherwise unknown or "hidden" fields were placed under the direct control of the governor-general, and at the same time, local taxes were raised and standardized in order to increase tax revenue. As mentioned earlier, based on the successful model of the opium consolidation system, a monopoly system was also introduced for salt, camphor, tobacco, and liquor. Although there were many detours along the way, the plan to end the receipt of government subsidies in the fiscal year 1902 was realized.

Taiwan's financial independence was achieved in 1907. This self-reliance continued until Japan's defeat in 1945, when it was forced to abandon Taiwan.

In addition, the government had to actively seek financial revenue. The proactive policy of Kodama and Gotō was to seek a way to develop the sugar industry in Taiwan. This was where Nitobe Inazō, the author of the best-selling English language book on Japan, *Bushido*, came in.

ONE WORD THAT MOVED NITOBE INAZŌ

While Nitobe was traveling in California for his health, he received a letter from Sone Arasuke, minister of agriculture and commerce, requesting him to work for the governor-general of Taiwan.[16] Nitobe replied that he could not accept the request because it was impossible for him to work in Taiwan in his condition. Sone's requests continued, and in his second request letter, he wrote that it was actually based on a strong desire by Kodama and Gotō. Gotō also sent Nitobe a long telegram. It was difficult for Nitobe to refuse the request from Gotō, who was also from his hometown (of Morioka in Aomori Prefecture) and who had already established a high reputation for his unique governing philosophy and administrative ability. The phrase of *shiki*, a Chinese historical record, "A warrior dies for those who know themselves," came to Nitobe's mind. After much deliberation, the author of *Bushido* decided he would go to Taiwan.

In order to be assigned to Taiwan, Nitobe needed to conduct further research on the colonial management of European countries, especially on tropical agriculture, and requested that he be given about one year to do so. The request was graciously granted by Gotō, having gotten his wish to have Nitobe join them. After one year of research, Nitobe returned to Japan in January 1901. He arrived in Tokyo via Kobe. There was an official at the train station to greet him. The official told him that Gotō had just arrived in Tokyo on business and would like for Nitobe to come see him.

Nitobe went to Gotō's private residence where he was lying in bed with a high fever due to influenza. It was his first meeting with Gotō. On February 2, Nitobe received a letter of appointment as a technician in the governor-general's office and left for Taiwan soon after. Gotō had already returned to Taipei and was extremely busy. In May, Nitobe was assigned as the head of the Industrial Promotion Division of the governor-general's office, where he was requested by Gotō to submit suggestions to improve the sugar industry immediately. He had only been in Taiwan for a little over three months, and his knowledge of the current situation in Taiwan was still very limited. He requested that he be allowed to observe the sugar industry in Java, which had already been established by the Dutch, if only for a month or so. Gotō agreed.

When he returned from Java, Gotō told him to write up his recommendations immediately. Nitobe responded he had only been in Java for about three weeks and had yet to thoroughly investigate Taiwan itself. To which Gotō said it would be better to write the suggestions before he know anything about the actual situation in Taiwan.

The more you study about Taiwan, the less you will be able to discern. You will become tired and not be able to come up with drastic improvements. Please write while your mind is still fresh dry from your travels in Java. I know it will be difficult, but I want you to draft it from high, with a big perspective.

For Nitobe, Gotō's words struck a chord with him. Gotō was fighting on the "policy" battlefield of Taiwan as an administrative "military strategist." What Gotō was looking for is not a scholarly paper. He had to find the best solution in the limited time he had. Nitobe made up his mind once again and devoted himself to writing the recommendations. Gotō handed the recommendations to Kodama after receiving them.

Speaking of strategists, Gotō's boss Kodama was one of the best military strategists. Nitobe was summoned to the governor-general's office. He found his written opinion on the desk. It seemed that Kodama had already read through everything. He was dressed in full military uniform, and though small in stature, he exuded an air of dignity. He sat Nitobe down on the sofa, while he stood and told him he had read his paper on the sugar industry twice:

I never read the same document twice, but the success of the sugar industry is key to Taiwan's financial independence, so I read it more carefully than I normally do. I have decided to go with it. If you have anything to add, let me know.

Nitobe was somewhat stunned, and said, "But the question is whether or not we can implement it as written. There is one part in the paper that I would like Your Excellency to read."

Kodama answered, "It is the part about Frederick the Great, right?" Nitobe responded,

Yes, exactly. The King implemented strict policies to reform Prussia's agricultural policy, sometimes using police powers and sometimes even the military police. I believe that if we want to make Taiwan financially independent based on the sugar industry, we need to be more determined than Frederick was. Having old-fashioned farmers plant improved seeds or using machines will not be easy. Even if His Excellency insists that we do it according to the recommendation, I, an engineer who has never led a single soldier, cannot do anything about it by myself. The whole issue depends on the Governor-General's decision, whether his Excellency will act on this opinion or not.[17]

Nitobe's forehead was dripping with sweat as he struggled to hold on. Kodama walked busily around the room three or four times before stopping in front of the sofa where Nitobe was sitting. "We'll do it," the governor-general told him.

In June 1902, a Provisional Taiwan Sugar Bureau was established with Nitobe as its director, and various regulations and bylaws were promulgated based on Nitobe's recommendations, marking the beginning of the modernization of Taiwan's sugar industry. The introduction of improved varieties from Java, the adoption of deep plowing methods, intensive farming with increased fertilizer use, the construction of water harvesting facilities, and the encouragement of land reclamation were all implemented.

Taiwan's indigenous sugarcane had been a poor crop with low yield, but through the free distribution of improved varieties, subsidies for fertilizer costs, and increased purchase prices, the industry began to show remarkable growth. The amount of sugar production from FY 1903 to FY 1910 exceeded Nitobe's bullish expectations. The same was true for the sugar consumption tax revenue. The area under cultivation for sweet crop production, which was 21,000 hectares in 1903, had increased to 125,700 hectares in 1917. The increase in sweet yield and the expansion of cultivated land led to the establishment of new sugar refineries, which marked the beginning of Taiwan's industrialization. The first sugar refinery in Taiwan was established in 1900 in Caiaotou—between Tainan and Kaohsiung—as the Taiwan Sugar

番子寮地方甘蔗灌漑試驗　　收量甲當 220,400斤（1 斤＝600G）（ 9寸灌漑）

Figure 6.6   Improved Sugarcane Field. *Source*: (from Wu, Kanan Taishū Kensetsu Kōtei Kankai)

Refining Company, with Mitsui and other mainland conglomerates as major shareholders, as a result of Gotō's persuasion, followed by the Ensuiko Sugar Refining Company.

GOTŌ'S ADMINISTRATIVE SKILLS

The development of the infrastructure, such as North-South Railway, going from Keelung to Kaohsiung, was vital to the success of these projects. And all of these projects were made possible by the issuance of Taiwan Project Public Bonds.

The first thing that Kodama and Gotō wanted to make happen was a longitudinal railroad connecting Taiwan from north to south. At the urging of the two men, the Railroad Department of the governor-general's office was established in November 1899, and Gotō became the first director of the department and took charge of the project.

What stands out in Gotō's administrative ability was the way he boldly selected people with superior skills and insights and entrusted them with complete confidence in the undertaking of his projects. This was the case with Nitobe Inazō in the development of the sugar industry and Nakamura Korekimi in the land surveys.

Similarly, Hasegawa Kinsuke was entrusted with the construction of the railroads. Although Hasegawa's talent as a railroad engineer was highly evaluated for the Tenryu River Bridge and the Yanagase Tunnel on the Hokuriku Line on Honshu in Japan, he could not stand the bureaucracy and ended up resigning from the government, becoming a nobleman. When Gotō heard about this, he took notice of Hasegawa, became enamored with him, and selected him to be the chief engineer of the Taiwan Railway Department.

In Taiwan, where bandits riddle the plains, savages are found in the mountains, and endemic diseases are rampant throughout, the task of constructing a north to south railroad from Keelung to Kaohsiung was an extremely difficult one. Hasegawa, who had gained Gotō's confidence, decided that he would take on this difficult project in Taiwan. Hasegawa, who had gained Gotō's confidence, went to Taiwan not only for his own sake but also for the that of Kodama, who was from his hometown, of Gotō, a bureaucrat and politician of the first rank in terms of insight, and for a great national project.

Early on, Gotō told Hasegawa, "My job is to get the budget. I will leave it up to you to make whatever plans you have to and get whatever you need within that budget." In fact, the project encountered many hardships, such as difficulties in purchasing materials and equipment, storms, the threat of endemic diseases, poor soil quality, a shortage of manpower, and the interruption of shipping, but Hasegawa overcame these difficulties with his unflagging spirit and resourcefulness. The construction was completed in April 1908, two years ahead of schedule.[18]

In October 1908, a ceremony was held to mark the completion of the railway. This was a short time after Gotō had been transferred to Dalian as the first president of the Manchuria Railway Company (*Mantetsu*).

Another major project was the construction of ports in Keelung and Kaohsiung. Taiwan is an island with few inlets and outlets along its coastline, and it is not easy to find good ports. Only Keelung in the northeastern part of Taiwan and Kaohsiung in the southwestern part of the island had deep inlets that could be further developed. However, both ports are subject to constant wind and waves, and the water depth was relatively shallow, internationally speaking. It was difficult for large ships to anchor, and thus they had to do so several kilometers offshore. It was essential to construct breakwaters and submerge the harbors. Without the construction of two harbors and the extension of the north-south railroad to this harbor, the development of Taiwan would not be able to truly begin.

The construction of the ports was considered one of the three most important projects in Taiwan, along with the building of the longitudinal railroad and the land survey project. The first phase of construction for Keelung Port began in 1899. The main work continued in the next phase, from 1906 to 1912. Nagao Hanpei, who was serving as the head of the Civil Engineering Section of the Civil Affairs Department of the governor-general's office, had the full trust of Gotō and was responsible for the second phase of the project.

Nagao, who was in his mid-thirties, took the project design to Kodama and Gotō and spent two hours explaining it to them. He was bombarded with detailed, reasonable questions from the governor-general and the Civil Affairs director general, and did his best to answer them. Kodama looked at Gotō and after giving his blessing, suggested they leave the project up to Nagao.

The matter was decided at once, and everything was left to Nagao, with no interference at all. Nagao, feeling enthusiastic, hurried to build the port according to the plan.

In 1900, Kodama was asked to become the Minister of War in the fourth Itō Hirobumi Cabinet in 1900, Minister of Home Affairs and concurrent Minister of Education in the Katsura Tarō Cabinet in 1903, and General of the Army in 1905. During the Russo-Japanese War, he became the chief of staff of the Manchurian Army and played a leading role in leading the war to victory. During this time, Kodama served simultaneously as governor-general of Taiwan but left matters to Gotō as the trusted civilian governor.

In November 1905, Kodama returned from Dalian, determined to continue his duties as governor-general of Taiwan. However, on July 23, 1906, as if the Russo-Japanese War had exhausted all his energy, he passed away peacefully in his sleep. He was fifty-four years old. Kodama's tenure as the fourth governor-general of Taiwan came to an end, and Sakuma Samata, a general in the army, was appointed as the new governor-general of Taiwan.

The day before his death, Kodama called Gotō and entrusted him with becoming the first president of the Manchuria Railway Company, the base for the development of Manchuria, Japan's next hope. In accordance with Kodama's wishes, Gotō became the president of Manchuria Railway Company on November 13 of the same year and resigned from his post as director general of the Taiwan governor-general's office's Civil Affairs Bureau. The era of the "Kodama-Gotō administration," as it was known in Japan, ended with Kodama's death and Gotō's appointment as the president of the South Manchuria Railway. Kodama's tenure as governor-general of Taiwan lasted eight years and two months, and Gotō's tenure as director general of the Civil Affairs Bureau lasted eight years and eight months.

NOTES

1. Gaimushō Nihon Gaikō Bunsho Digital Archives 1895, Vol. 28, No. 2.
2. Ibid.
3. Itō, *Taiwan*, and Kō, *Taiwan Sōtokufu*.
4. Kobayashi Michihiko, *Kodama Gentarō: Soko Kara Ryojun ha Mieru ka* (Kodama Gentarō: Can You See Port Arthur from There?) (Kyōto: Minerva Shobō, 2012), and Chōnan Masayoshi, *Kodama Gentarō* (Tokyo: Sakuhinsha, 2019).
5. Yamaoka Junichirō, *Gotō Shinpei: Nihon no Rashinban to Natta Otoko* (Gotō Shinpei: The Man Who Became Japan's Compass) (Tokyo: Shisōsha, 2014).
6. Tsurumi Yūsuke (revised edition edited by Ikkai Tomoyoshi), *Seiden Gotō Shinpei Ketteiban 3 Taiwan Jidai* (Official Biography of Gotō Shinpei, Vol. 3: The Taiwan Years) (Tokyo: Fujiwara Shoten, 2005).
7. Ibid.
8. Ibid.
9. Ibid.
10. Gotō Shinpei, *Kokka Eisei Genri* (Principles of National Hygiene), 1890, in Gotō Shinpei Related Papers, National Diet Library Digital Archives.
11. Ibid.
12. Ibid.
13. This translation comes from Kitaoka Shinichi (translated by Iain Arthy), *Gotō Shinpei: Statesman of Vision Research, Public Health, and Development* (Tokyo: JPIC, 2021), p. 49.
14. Tsurumi, *Seiden Gotō Shinpei*,
15. Ibid.
16. Ibid.
17. Ibid.
18. Nakahama Takehiko, *Kaitaku Tetsudō ni Noseta Messeji: Tetsudōin Fukusōsai Hasegawa Kinsuke no Shōgai* (A Message Entrusted with the Development Railway: The Life of Ministry of Railways Vice President Hasegawa Kinsuke) (Tokyo: Fuzanbō International, 2016) and Hasegawa Hakase Hensan Iinkai, ed., *Kōgaku Hakase Hasegawa Kinsukeden* (A Biography of Hasegawa Kinsuke, Doctor of Engineering) (Tokyo: Hasegawa Hakaseden Hensankai, 1937).

Chapter 7

How England and the United States Saw Japan's Administration of Taiwan

REPRESENTATIVE MEDIA IN THE UNITED STATES AND EUROPE PRAISED IT

How should we evaluate the period of the formation of the foundation for the administration of Taiwan by Kodama and Gotō? How did the world, especially the West, view it? An article in a British newspaper, *The Times* (London), dated September 24, 1904, can help us understand these questions. It was reprinted the following day in the American paper, the *New York Times*.

Although the name of the reporter is not specified, judging from its excellent English and rich content, the article must have been written by a skilled correspondent who made detailed observations of Taiwan and conducted frequent interviews with the U.S. consulate and the governor-general's office. The fact that this article was published as a 2,400-word commentary in two leading Western newspapers is a good example to show how Japan's administration of Taiwan was evaluated in Britain and the United States at the time.

September 1905, the time when the article was published, was near the end of the Kodama–Gotō era. A decade earlier, the Treaty of Shimonoseki between Japan and China of April 1895 gave Japan legal possession of Taiwan. Kodama arrived as governor-general in February 1898, and Gotō became director-general of the Civil Affairs Bureau in June of the same year. What did Japan accomplish in Taiwan in such a short period of time, nine years and five months from the time it took possession of the island and six

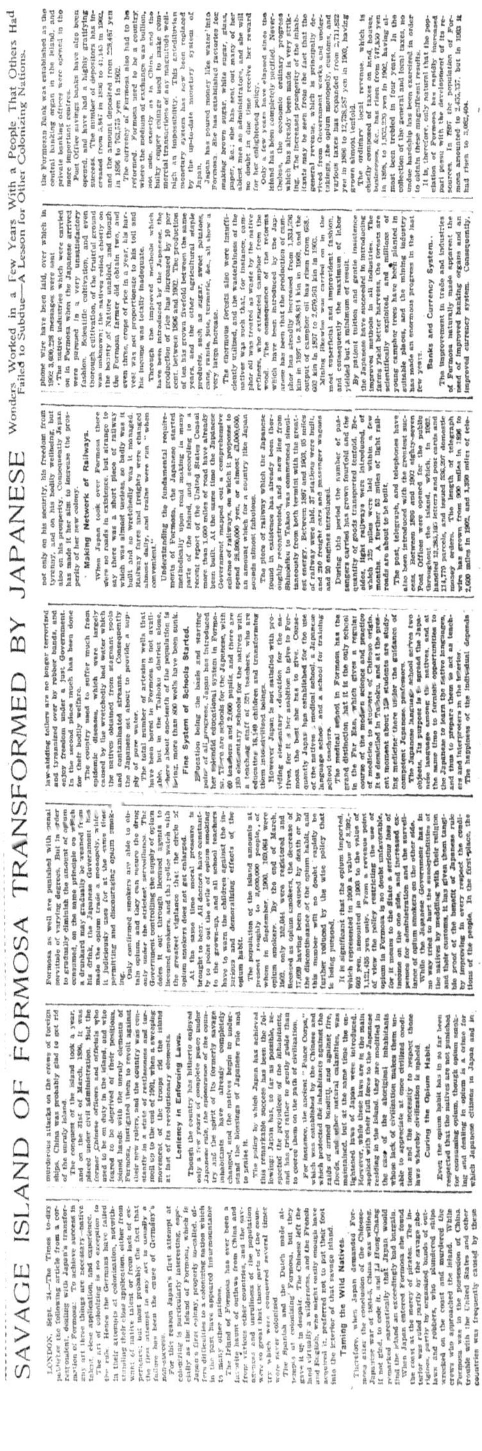

Figure 7.1 *New York Times Story about Taiwan under Japanese Administration. Source: (New York Times story from September 1924.)*

years and a few months from the arrival of Kodama and Gotō? It is worth reading an independent assessment, such as that provided by this article.

The title of the long commentary is "Savage Island of Formosa Transformed by Japanese: Wonders Worked in a Few Years with a People That Others Had Failed to Subdue—A Lesson for Other Colonizing Nations." The complete article is below.

LONDON, Sept. 24.-*The Times* to-day publishes the following article from a correspondent, dealing with Japan's transformation of Formosa: To achieve success in any art, three things are necessary—talent, close application, and experience.

The art of colonizing is no exception to the rule. Hence the Germans have failed in their attempts at colonization, notwithstanding their close application, either from want of native talent or from lack of experience; but most probably the fact that the first attempt in any art is usually a failure has been the cause of Germany's non-success.

For this reason, Japan's first attempt at colonizing is particularly interesting, especially as the Island of Formosa, which is Japan's first colony, properly so-called, offers difficulties to a colonizing nation which in the past may have appeared insurmountable to many other nations.

The Island of Formosa has ever been a favorite haunt of outlaws from China and from various other countries, and the savageness and unruliness of the population were so great that those parts of the country which were conquered several times were never colonized.

The Spanish and the Dutch made attempts at colonizing Formosa, but they gave it up in despair. The Chinese left the land virtually a wilderness, and the French and English, who might easily enough have acquired it, preferred not to put their foot into the interior of that savage island.

TAMING THE WILD NATIVES

Therefore, when Japan demanded Formosa after the conclusion of the Chinese-Japanese war of 1894–1985, China was willing, if not glad, to cede it, and Li Hung-Chang remarked sarcastically that Japan would find the island an exceedingly bad bargain.

When Japan entered Formosa, she found the coast at the mercy of pirates. The interior was ruled partly by the savage aborigines, partly by organized bands of outlaws and robbers, who plundered ships wrecked on the coast and murdered the crews who approached the island. While Formosa was in the possession of China, trouble with the United States and other countries was frequently caused by these murderous attacks on the crews of foreign ships. China was probably glad to get rid of the unruly island.

The conquest of the island took a year, and on the 31st of March, 1896, it was placed under civil administration. But the former Chinese officers and officials

Chapter 7

who used to be on duty in the island, and who feared to be deprived of their positions, joined hands with the unruly elements of Formosa, instigated them to revolt against their new rulers, and the country was constantly in a state of restlessness and turmoil up to the end of 1901, when a sweeping movement of the troops rid the island at last of its revolutionary elements.

LENIENCY IN ENFORCING LAWS

Though the country has hitherto enjoyed only a few years of complete peace under Japanese rule, the appearance of the country and the spirit of its formerly savage inhabitants have already completely changed, and the natives begin to understand the blessings of Japanese rule and to praise it.

The policy by which Japan has achieved this remarkable success has been the following: Japan has, so far as possible, respected the prejudices of the inhabitants, and has tried rather to gently guide than to coerce them on the path of civilization.

For instance, the ancient "Peace Corps," which was established by the Chinese and which protected the inhabitants against the raids of armed banditti, and against fire, floods, and other natural calamities, was maintained, but at the same time, the enlightened laws of Japan were introduced. However, while these laws are in the main applied with their full force to the Japanese residing in the island, they are modified in the case of the aboriginal inhabitants whose lack of civilization makes them unable to appreciate at once civilized conditions and the necessity to respect those laws whereby civilization is upheld.

CURING THE OPIUM HABIT

Even the opium habit has in so far been respected that the natives are not punished for consuming opium, though opium smoking and dealing in opium is a crime for which Japanese citizens in Japan and in Formosa as well are punished with penal servitude of varying degrees. But in order to gradually diminish the amount of opium consumed, on the same principle on which a drunkard may gradually be weaned from his drink, the Japanese Government has made the opium trade a monopoly, which it judiciously uses for at the same time permitting and discouraging opium smoking.

Only confirmed smokers are able to obtain opium, and they can secure the drug only under the strictest surveillance. The Government controlling the supply of opium doles it out through licensed agents to licensed smokers, and the police watch with the greatest vigilance that the circle of opium smokers does not get enlarged.

At the same time, moral pressure is brought to bear. All doctors have constantly to point out the evils of opium smoking to the grown-up, and all school teachers have to warn the children against the injurious and demoralizing effects of the opium habit.

The population of the island amounts at present roughly to 3,000,000 people, of whom, in September, 1900, 169,064 were opium smokers. By the end of March, 1902, only 152,044 were registered and licensed as opium smokers, the decrease of 17,020 having been caused by death or by the discontinuance of the opium habit, and this number will no doubt rapidly be further reduced by the wise policy that is being pursued.

It is significant that the opium imported, which represented in 1900 a value of 3,392, 602 yen, amounted in 1903 to the value of 1,121,455 yen only. From a revenue point of view, the policy restricting the use of opium in Formosa is no doubt unfavorable, for it means to the State a serious loss of income, on the one side, and increased expenses for administration and the surveillance of opium smokers, on the other side.

While the Japanese Government has in no way tried to hurt the susceptibilities of the natives by meddling with their religion and their customs, it has given them tangible proof of the benefit of Japanese rule by improving in every respect the conditions of the people. In the first place, the law-abiding toilers are no longer tyrannized over by robber bands and enjoy freedom under a just Government. In the second place, much has been done for their bodily welfare.

The country used to suffer much from epidemic diseases, which were largely caused by the wretchedly bad water which the natives obtained from stagnant pools and contaminated streams. Consequently, the Japanese set about to provide a supply of pure water.

The total number of artesian wells that have been bored in Formosa is not available, but in the Taihoku district alone, where about one-tenth of the population is living, more than 800 wells have been sunk.

FINE SYSTEM OF SCHOOLS STARTED

Education being the basis and starting point of all progress, Japan has introduced her splendid educational system in Formosa. There are schools for the Japanese, with 60 teachers and 2,000 pupils and there are 130 elementary schools for the natives with a teaching staff of 521 teachers, who are educating 18,149 children and transforming them into civilized beings.

However, Japan is not satisfied with providing elementary education for the natives, for it is her ambition to give to Formosa the best she has to give. Consequently, Japan has established for the use of the natives a medical school, a Japanese language school, and a school for training school teachers.

The medical school in Formosa has the grand distinction that it is the only school in the Far East which gives a regular course of the modern science and practice of medicine to students of Chinese origin. It is domiciled in Taihoku, and at the present moment, about 150 students are studying medicine there under the guidance of competent Japanese professors.

The Japanese language school serves two objects. Its purpose is to spread the Japanese language among the natives, and at the same time to furnish opportunities to the Japanese to learn the native languages, and thus to prepare them to act as teachers and interpreters in the interior.

The happiness of the individual depends not only on his security, his freedom from tyranny, and on his bodily wellbeing but also on his prosperity. Consequently, Japan has made it her aim to increase the prosperity of her new colony.

MAKING NETWORK OF RAILWAYS

When Japan took over Formosa, there were no roads in existence, but strange to say there was a short piece of railway which was almost useless, so badly was it built and so wretchedly was it managed. Railway fares and freights were changed almost daily, and trains were run "when convenient."

Understanding the fundamental requirements of Formosa, the Japanese started methodically upon road making in many parts of the island, and according to a recent report of the United States Consul, more than 1000 miles of road have already been built. At the same time, the Japanese Government mapped out a comprehensive scheme of railways, on which it proposes to spend 28,800,000 yen, or almost £3,000,000, an amount which for a country like Japan sounds almost fabulous.

The piece of railway which the Japanese found in existence has already been thoroughly reconstructed, and a new line from Shinchiku to Takao was commenced simultaneously from both termini with the greatest energy. Between 1907 and 1908, 95 miles of railway were laid, 37 stations were built, and 210 freight cars and passenger wagons and 20 engines introduced.

During this period, the number of passengers carried has grown fourfold and the quantity of goods transported tenfold. Besides, light railways were introduced, of which 125 miles were laid within a few months. A further 52 miles of light railroads are about to be built.

The post, telegraph, and telephones have also been introduced with the greatest success. Between 1896 and 1903, eighty-seven Post Offices were opened for the public throughout the island, which, in 1902, handled 13,285,105 letters and post cards and 114,779 parcels, and issued 336,207 domestic money orders. The length of telegraph wire has grown from 900 miles in 1896 to 2,600 miles in 1902, and 1,350 miles of telephone wire have been laid, over which in 1902, 3,690,228 messages were sent.

The native industries which were carried on in Formosa when the Japanese arrived were pursued in a very unsatisfactory fashion. Scientific cultivation and even thorough cultivation, of the fruitful ground was unknown; the natives relied chiefly on the bounty of Nature unaided, and though the Formosa farmer did obtain two, and even three, crops of rice in a year, his harvest was not proportionate to his toil and his income was totally inadequate.

Through the improved methods which have been introduced by the Japanese, the production of rice has increased by 10 percent between 1896 and 1902. The production of tea has grown fivefold between the same years, and the other agricultural staple products, such as sugar, sweet potatoes, cane, ramie, jute, turmeric, &c., all show a very large increase.

The enormous forests also were insufficiently utilized, and the wastefulness of the natives was such that, for instance, camphor oil was treated as waste by the native refiners. who extracted camphor from the wood. The consequence of the reforms which have been introduced by the Japanese has been that the production of camphor has steadily increased from 1,534,596 kin in 1897 to 3,588,814 kin in 1903, and the output of camphor oil has risen from 638,603 kin in 1897 to 2,670,501 kin in 1903.

Mining likewise was carried on in the most superficial and improvident fashion, and consequently the maximum of labor yielded but a minimum of result.

By patient tuition and gentle insistence, the Japanese have succeeded in introducing improved methods in all industries. The farms yield better harvests, the forests are scientifically exploited, and millions of young camphor trees have been planted in suitable places, and the mining industry has made an enormous progress in the last few years.

BANKS AND CURRENCY SYSTEM

The improvement in trade and industries of Formosa naturally made apparent the need of improved banking organs and an improved currency system. Consequently, the Formosan Bank was established as the central banking organ in the island, and private banking offices were opened in the more important centres.

Post Office savings banks have also been opened and have had a highly gratifying success. The number of depositors has increased from 5,847 in 1896 to 41,145 in 1902, and the amount deposited from 228,487 yen in 1896 to 763,575 yen in 1902.

The currency of Formosa also had to be reformed. Formosa used to be a country where the medium of exchange was bullion, not coin, exactly as in China, and the bulky copper coinage used to make commercial transactions of any magnitude well-nigh an impossibility. This antediluvian monetary system has now been replaced by the up-to-date monetary system of Japan.

Japan has poured money like water into Formosa. She has established factories for making brown sugar, white sugar, glass, paper, &c.; she has sent out many of her ablest men as administrators, and she will no doubt in due time receive her reward for her enlightened policy.

Only a few years have elapsed since the island has been completely pacified. Nevertheless, the economic ordinary progress which has already been made is very striking. The increased prosperity of the inhabitants may be seen from the fact that the general revenue, which is principally derived from Government works and undertakings, the opium monopoly, customs, and various taxes has expanded from 2,711,822 yen in 1898 to 12,739,587 yen in 1902, having grown almost tenfold.

The ordinary local revenue, which is chiefly composed of taxes on land, houses, businesses, &c., has risen from 747,850 yen in 1898 to 1,952,220 yen in 1903, having almost trebled in four years. In the collection of the general and local taxes, no undue hardship has been exercised in order to obtain these magnificent results.

It is, therefore, only natural that the population of Formosa has rapidly increased *parl passu* with the development of its resources. In 1897, the population of Formosa amounted to 2,455,357, but in 1903, it had risen to 3,082,404.

TAIWANESE SECONDARY SCHOOL TEXTBOOK, "UNDERSTANDING TAIWAN"

How did the local residents of Taiwan perceive the era of Japan's administration? In order to understand this, we need to look at how the era of Japanese rule was taught at the secondary school (junior high school) level. There is no better place to start than with the standard history textbook for secondary schools titled, *Renshi Taiwan,* or "Understanding Taiwan," which was developed during the political democratization process under the late former President Lee Teng-hui and has been used throughout Taiwan since 1997.[1]

This textbook became part of the social studies program after the restructuring of the curriculum under the Chen Shui-chiang administration in 2008, and although the descriptions are no longer the same, the content is still similar to that of "Understanding Taiwan." Here, we will look at the descriptions of the Japanese administration of Taiwan.

In the section on "Social Changes" during the Japanese administration, the textbook covers five topics: (1) rapid growth of the population, (2) universalization of the ban on bound feet and queue (pigtail) hair, (3) fostering punctuality, (4) establishment of a law-abiding mentality, and (5) the establishment of modern hygiene.

The book explains the establishment of a law-abiding spirit as follows:

> The Governor-General used the police and *hokō* system to achieve effective social control, strictly reduce crime and maintain order, and prevent the people from breaking the law out of spite. At the same time, through schools and social education, the modern concept of the rule of law and knowledge were injected into the people so that they would learn to respect order and law, and in addition, the judiciary earned the trust of the public by maintaining justice and righteousness, and this influence helped the people to develop habits such as being at ease with the law and observing discipline, and to establish a law-abiding spirit.[2]

Viewed from the perspectives of economic, social, and cultural development, Japan's administration of Taiwan is a far more successful example than any of the colonies of the West. This is a clear indication of the high

Figure 7.2   Cover of a Taiwan History Textbook. *Source*: (from Kokuritsu Henyakukan)

aspirations of the Japanese leaders involved in Taiwan's governance during the Meiji era. Japan's administration of Taiwan was clearly not aimed at exploitation and deprivation like the colonial rule of the other Powers. It was the transplantation of Japan's model of modern civilization to Taiwan while taking into consideration local habits and customs, and the spirit of this transplantation and guiding approach was to demonstrate to the world the nature of Imperial Japan.

In his outstanding work on Japan's colonial history, the late historian Mark R. Peattie discussed the question of Japan's motivations in administering Taiwan. His scholarship, published more than forty years ago, is worth reading for its objective analysis:

> I have spoken of the maritime tropical empires of the West as the pattern for the overseas empire which Japan assembled between 1895 and 1922. In a general as well as a symbolic sense, this is true, for the trappings of the Japanese colonial presence and life-style were indeed Western in appearance. But the framework of colonial *policy* as it was formed in the first half of the empire was less modelled on direct European precedents than on the superbly successful modernization effort which Japan had undertaken in the three decades after the Meiji leadership had overthrown the Tokugawa feudal order, a reform program based in large part, of course, on Western experience. It is not too much to say that Japanese colonialism in its formative stage cannot be understood outside the perimeters of *fukoku-kyōhei*—that collective exhortation of early Meiji that bound all of Japan's modernizing reforms to the twin goals of a strong and prosperous Japan. All that Japan undertook in its colonies during the first quarter century of the empire was based upon Meiji experience in domestic reform.[3]

Contributing to the advancement of developing countries remains an important diplomatic task for Japan. In undertaking this today, we should explore the origin of "development studies" as found in the administrative ideas and concepts spread by Gotō Shinpei and others and refine them as Japan's own unique approach to development policies in global history.

NOTES

1. Kokuritsu Henyakukan, ed. (Sai Ekitatsu and Nagayama Hideki [trans.]), *Taiwan o Shiru: Taiwan Kokumin Chūgaku Rekishi Kyōkasho* (Knowing Taiwan: Taiwan National Middle School History Textbook, 2000).

2. Ibid.

3. Raymon H. Myers and Mark R. Peattie, *The Japanese Colonial Empire, 1895–1945* (Princeton: Princeton University Press, 1987), p. 23.

Conclusion

Why Korea is "Anti-Japanese" and Taiwan "Pro-Japanese"

I am often asked (and more and more so recently) why Korea is "anti-Japanese" and Taiwan so favorable to Japan. My response is: "If you look at the beginning of modern history how Japan became involved with the two territories, you will understand."

Taiwan was an overseas territory ceded to Japan by the Qing Dynasty after Japan's victory in the Sino-Japanese War. At the time Japan set foot on Taiwan, the island was inhabited by those of Malays, Polynesian natives, and ethnic groups with different languages and customs who had migrated from Fujian and Guangdong on the other side of the straight, making Taiwan a heterogeneous place. The tribes from the mainland drove the indigenous people into the mountainous areas and mutually competed with each other for land and control. This is known as a "classification struggle." The term "classification" referred to people with different origins, and "struggle" refers to fighting and conflict. Tropical diseases such as cholera and plague were also prevalent.

In 1683, the Qing government made Taiwan its own territory as the Taiwan Office of Fujian Province. However, the Qing government was not interested in the development of Taiwan and left it as an "uncivilized land" that was not subject to the virtue of the *tianzi* (emperor). Japan came to possess an island that was devoid of a political structure and social integration. In order to begin its rule, Japan first had to eliminate the anti-Japanese forces, an outlaw group called "local bandits," consisting of Qing soldiers and local residents. The resistance was not organized, per se, but it was intense. Japan had no choice but to fight "another Sino-Japanese war" in Taiwan. What awaited Japan after it succeeded in conquering the island was tropical disease and the "Opium scourge" that deeply affected the margins of society. Taiwan was literally an "intractable island."

It was not until the fourth Japanese governor-general of Taiwan, Kodama Gentarō, and the director for Civil Affairs, Gotō Shinpei, assumed their positions that Taiwan's development began to take off. Taiwan had no long history or rich culture to speak of to inherit. However, this meant that once the initial difficulties were overcome, there was no barrier to subsequent development. In fact, Kodama and Gotō proceeded with development according to their own design and were able to achieve the island's social integration in every corner of the island for the first time in its history. From then on, until the "abandonment" of Taiwan due to Japan's defeat in World War II, Japan instilled its social order and social norms in Taiwan. After the abandonment of Taiwan, the social order and social norms of the Japanese era appeared to have had collapsed under the harsh politics of the Kuomintang (KMT) Nationalist Party, which occupied Taiwan, particularly during the thirty-eight years of martial law. However, with the advent of the Japanese-speaking, Japan-educated President Lee Teng-hui's democratization era, the social order and social norms of the Japanese era were vividly revived and became the source of Taiwan's modern identity.

The history of Korea, on the other hand, greatly differed. For more than 500 years prior to the Japanese occupation of the Korean Peninsula, Korea was ruled rigidly under the Joseon Dynasty. During this period, the ruling gentry, or "Yangban," were strongly influenced by Chinese ideology. They believed they were a "little China." Although they were subservient to the Qing Dynasty, they believed that the mainstream of China was not in the Qing Dynasty—the conquering Manchus—but in Joseon (Korea). They felt that Joseon was more Chinese than China, and that they were a purer version of China. Japan, on the other hand, was regarded as a "barbarian" with no morality or justice, far inferior to that of Joseon. As it turned out, Korea would be annexed by this barbarian, Japan.

The Joseon Dynasty was an overwhelmingly hierarchical state based on the principles of orthodox neo-Confucianism. Wives obeyed their husbands, children obeyed their parents, and those of lower status obeyed those of higher status. When this family morality becomes the political morality, the people have no other way to live but to blindly follow the elite surrounding the king. If this type of society becomes the basis for political governance, it becomes a one-party despotic state. There were only "those who take and those from who are taken" in Joseon during this period. There was no middle class at all. It was Japan that brought in the abolition of the status system, the inviolability of "private property," and the principle of freedom of contract. These reforms greatly impacted the vested interests of the ruling elite, and thus Japanese rule became intensely unacceptable to them.

With Japan's defeat in World War II, it had to abandon its rule over Korea. However, a mere three decades of control was not enough to dispel the

notions that had persisted for over 500 years in Korea. The Korean intellectu-
als, leftist scholars, political and bureaucratic elite of today are unmistakably
the latest incarnation of the "ruling gentry" in this view. Those that collabo-
rated with Japan during its rule of the peninsula were not liquidated, and the
independence activists did not become the main players in the founding of
the country. The new rulers of Korea, anti-Communist Syngman Rhee and
Park Chung-hee, chose the path of a divided Korea and created the Republic
of Korea in partnership with Japan, which had invaded Korea, and the United
States, which was allied with Japan. In many quarters, this was morally inex-
cusable. This is no doubt how the current president, Moon Jae-in, must feel.
To stop being anti-Japanese would be to dismiss their own legitimacy. The
elites believe that Korea is a "wrongly created country," according to Dr. Lee
Young-hoon, a critic of what he calls "Anti-Japanese Tribalism."[1] It certainly
seems so. The phrases, "reckoning with the past" and "reckoning with the
accumulated damage" are political terms matching their sentiments.

In response to South Korea's constant criticisms, Japan should just respond
with the objective facts.

With regard to Taiwan, Japan cannot simply expect Taiwan to be pro-
Japan. Japan must engage better diplomatically.

In the 2020 presidential election, Tsai Ing-wen of the Democratic
Progressive Party won re-election by defeating her KMT opponent Han
Kuo-yu, earning the most votes ever. Immediately after, she held a press
conference and said, "Democratic Taiwan and the government elected by the
people will not succumb to blackmail. Beijing must understand this." In an
interview with the BBC, she added, "We do not need to declare ourselves
an independent nation. We are already an independent nation, and we call
ourselves Taiwan, Republic of China."

Her most important issue is how to secure the space for Taiwan's own
survival in light of China's expanding influence. Taiwan is struggling with
foreign policy challenges that would be hard to imagine in other countries,
such as Japan, which enjoys a peaceful diplomatic environment thanks to the
Japan-U.S. alliance without any major political rivalry. Taiwan today is facing the enormous pressures from China that Japan will sooner or later have
to face itself.

The contents of this book first appeared in installments in the monthly magazine, *Seiron*, published in Japan, over the course of one year. It was meant
to contribute to the Japanese people's understanding of the history of Japan's
involvement with Taiwan. Due to the popularity of the series, I decided to
publish it in book form and did the necessary rewrites and corrections.

I am very grateful for the assistance of Ishizaki Rie of the executive secretary's office at Takushoku University in collecting materials and illustra-
tions. I am also grateful to Ichikawa Yūji of Sankei Shimbun Publishing

Co., Ltd., did a meticulous job of editing the entire book, even down to its reorganization.

Watanabe Toshio

Spring 2020

POSTSCRIPT TO THE ENGLISH EDITION

Shortly after the original version appeared in Japanese, Dr. Robert D. Eldridge, a longtime resident of Japan and supporter of strengthening Taiwan-Japan-U.S. cooperation, approached me about translating the book into English. Having known him and his research for many years and excited at the prospect, I readily agreed. I would like to thank him for his suggestion, his efforts at translation, and his coordination with the U.S. publisher.

Watanabe Toshio

July 2021

NOTE

1. His book was originally published in Korea, followed by Japan, in 2019 and immediately became a best seller. No English version currently exists, but if it did, the title (of the Japanese version) would read in English: *Anti-Japanese Tribalism: Sources of Crisis between Japan and Korea.*

Bibliography

Chōnan, Masayoshi. *Kodama Gentarō* (Tokyo: Sakuhinsha, 2019).

Dalyrmple, Dana G. *Development and Spread of High-Yielding Wheat Varieties in Developing Countries* (Washington, DC: Agency for International Development, 1986)

Furukawa, Katsumi. *Taiwan o Aishita Nihonjin: Hatta Yoichi no Shōgai* (A Japanese Man Who Loved Taiwan: The Life of Hatta Yoichi) (Tokyo: Sōfūsha, 2009).

Gotō, Shinpei. *Kokka Eisei Genri* (Principles of National Hygiene), 1890.

Hasegawa Hakase Hensan Iinkai, ed. *Kōgaku Hakase Hasegawa Kinsukeden* (A Biography of Hasegawa Kinsuke, Doctor of Engineering) (Tokyo: Hasegawa Hakaseden Hensankai, 1937).

Hatta Gishi Fusai o Shitai Taiwan to Yūkō no Kai, ed. *Mizu Akari: Hatta Yoichi Zuishiroku* (Faint Reflection of Light on Water in the Dark: Various Memories of Hatta Yoichi) (Kanazawa: Hokkoku Shimbunsha, 2020).

Hayami, Yūjirō. *Development Economics: From the Poverty to the Wealth of Nations* (Oxford: Clarendon Press, 1997).

Hokkoku Shimbunsha Shuppankyoku, ed. *Kaisō no Hatta Yoichi: Ichikazoku Ya Yukari no Hito no Shōgen de Tsuzuru* (Reflections of Hatta Yoichi: Family and Those with a Connection Remember Him) (Kanazawa: Hokkoku Shimbunsha, 2016).

Inaba, Kikuo. *Baruton Sensei, Meiji Nihon o Kakeru* (Teacher Burton, Racing Around Meiji Japan) (Tokyo: Heibonsha, 2016).

Inaba, Kikuo. *Toshi no Ishi: Hamano Yashirō no Kiseki* (City Doctor: The Story of Hamano Yashirō) (Tokyo: Suidō Sangyō Shimbunsha, 1993).

Iso Eikichi Zuisōroku (Iso Eikichi's Random Thoughts), (privately published, 1974).

Itō, Kiyoshi. *Taiwan: 400 Nen no Rekishi to Tenbō* (Taiwan: Four Hundred Years of History and Its Prospects) (Tokyo: Chūō Kōronsha, 1993).

Kai, Jun. *Hatta Yoichi no Tsuma: Taiwan ni Tōyōichi no Damu o Tsukutta Hatta Gishi no Tsuma* (Hatta Yoichi's Wife: The Wife of the Engineer Who Made the Greatest Dam in the Orient) (Tokyo: Tsuge Shobō, 2017).

159

Kitaoka, Shinichi (translated by Iain Arthy). *Gotō Shinpei: Statesman of Vision Research, Public Health, and Development* (Tokyo: JPIC, 2021).

Kobayashi, Michihiko. *Kodama Gentarō: Soko Kara Ryojun ha Mieru ka* (Kodama Gentarō: Can You See Port Arthur from There?) (Kyōto: Minerva Shobō, 2012).

Kokuritsu Henyakukan, ed. (Sai Ekitatsu and Nagayama Hideki [trans.]). *Taiwan o Shiru: Taiwan Kokumin Chūgaku Rekishi Kyōkasho* (Knowing Taiwan: Taiwan National Middle School History Textbook), 2000.

Kōkyō Hishū Kanan Taishū Kumiai. *Kōkyō Hishū Kanan Taishū Shinsetsu Jigyō Gaiyō* (Outline of the Public Waterworks Chianan Irrigation New Construction Project), 1930.

Ko, Se-kai. *Nihon Tōchika no Taiwan: Teikō to Danatsu* (Taiwan Under Japanese Administration: Resistance and Oppression) (Tokyo: Tōkyō Daigaku Shuppankai, 1972).

Kyūba, Kazutake and Watanabe Tadayo. "Shizen to Nōkō (Nature and Farming)," in Yano Tōru, ed., *Tōnan Ajiagaku e no Shōtai* (An Invitation to Southeast Asian Studies) (Tokyo: NHK Shuppankai, 1977).

Nakahama, Takehiko. *Kaitaku Tetsudō ni Noseta Messeji: Tetsudōin Fukusōsai Hasegawa Kinsuke no Shōgai* (A Message Entrusted with the Development Railway: The Life of Ministry of Railways Vice President Hasegawa Kinsuke) (Tokyo: Fuzanbō International, 2016).

Ng, Chiau-tong. *Taiwan Sōtokufu* (The Governor-General's Office in Taiwan) (Tokyo: Kyōikusha Rekishi Shinsho, 1981, republished in 2019 by Chikuma Shobō).

Myers, Raymon H., and Mark R. Peattie. *The Japanese Colonial Empire, 1895-1945* (Princeton: Princeton University Press, 1987).

Ō Sūkō. "Daichūkaka, Taiwan, Shōkoku Kaminka (Taiwan, Part of a Greater China or a Small Country in and of Itself)," in Kasahara Masaharu and Ueno Hiroko, eds., *Taiwan* (Tokyo: Kawade Shobō Shinsha, 1995).

Papers of Inoue Kaoru, National Diet Library, Tokyo, Japan.

Saigyō. *Saigyō Hōshi Kashū* (Collection of Poetry of Saigyō the Monk).

Shiba, Ryōtarō. *Suku no Ue no Kumo*, Vol. 1 (Tokyo: Bungei Shunjū, 1999), translation by Juliet Winters Carpenter and Paul McCarthy (edited by Phyllis Bimbaum), *Clouds Above the Hill* (London: Routledge, 2013).

Sugiyama, Mitsumaru. *Griin Fazaa: Indo no Sabaku o Midori ni Kaeta Nihonjin, Sugiyama Tatsumaru no Kiseki* (Green Father: Sugiyama Tatsumaru, The Japanese Man Who Was Responsible for Changing a Desert into a Green Area) (Hamamatsu City, Shizuoka Prefecture: Hikumano Shuppan, 2001).

Sugiyama, Tatsumaru. *Indo o Aruite: Ganji Ō no Ato o Tsugu Hitobito* (Walking India: The People Who Have Succeeded the Revered Ganji) (Fukuoka: Kokusai Bunka Fukushi Kyōkai, 1966).

Sugiyama, Tatsumaru. *Kiga o Ikiru Hitobito: Ganji Ō no Undō to ha Nani ka* (People Who Live With Starvation: What Was the Revered Ganji's Movement About?) (Tokyo: Ushio Shuppan, 1973).

Sugiyama, Tatsumaru. *Sabaku Ryokka ni Nozomu* (Trying to Turn a Desert Green) (Fukuoka: Ashi Shobō, 1984).

Taihoku Beikoku Jimusho, ed. *Kanan Taishū: Beikoku Jimusho Chōsa* (Chianan Irrigation: Office of Rice and Wheat Study), 1936.

Taiwan Rekishi Chizu Zōteiban (Revised and Expanded Edition of Taiwan History Map) (Taipei: Kokuritsu Taiwan Rekishi Hakubutsukan, undated).

Taiwan Suidōshi (Taiwan Waterworks Magazine).

Tsurumi, Yūsuke (revised edition edited by Ikkai Tomoyoshi). *Seiden Gotō Shinpei Ketteiban 3 Taiwan Jidai* (Official Biography of Gotō Shinpei, Vol. 3: The Taiwan Years) (Tokyo: Fujiwara Shoten, 2005).

Tsutsumi, Kazuyuki. "1910 Nendai Taiwan no Beishu Kairyō Keikaku to Suenaga Megumu (Suenaga Megumu and the Plan to Improve Rice Varieties in Taiwan in the 1910s)," *Tōyō Shihō*, No. 12: 12–24 (March 2006).

Watanabe, Toshio. *Gotō Shinpei no Taiwan: Jinrui mo Mata Seibutsu no Hitotsu Nari* (Gotō Shinpei's Taiwan: Improving Colonial Administration Through the Application of Biological Principles) (Tokyo: Chūō Kōron Shinsha, 2021).

Watanabe, Toshio. *Kaihatsu Keizaigaku Nyūmon* (An Introduction to Development Economics) (Tokyo: Tōyō Keizai Shinpōsha, 2010).

Watanabe, Toshio. *Kaihatsu Keizaigaku: Keizaigaku to Gendai Ajia* (Development Economics: Modern Asia and Economics) (Tokyo: Nihon Hyōronsha, 1986).

Watanabe, Toshio. *Watashi no Naka no Ajia* (The Asia in Me) (Tokyo: Chūō Kōron Shinsha, 2004).

Wu, Ming Yun. *Kanan Taishū Kensetsu Kōtei Kankai* (Introduction of Construction Process of Chianan Irrigation Construction Project), 1998.

Yamaoka, Junichirō. *Gotō Shinpei: Nihon no Rashinban to Natta Otoko* (Gotō Shinpei: The Man Who Became Japan's Compass) (Tokyo: Shisōsha, 2014).

Index

About the Author and Translator

ABOUT THE AUTHOR

Toshio Watanabe was born in Yamanashi Prefecture in 1939 and attended Keio University for his undergraduate and graduate school years. He received his doctorate in economics, specializing in the developing economies of postwar Asia. He has been a professor at Tsukaba University and Tokyo University of Technology, and has served as professor, president, and chancellor of Takushoku University. He has held leading positions in numerous foundations, government committees, and academic associations and is chairman of the Friends of Lee Teng-hui Association in Japan. His books include *Asia, Its Growth and Agony* (1992) and in Japanese, *Studies in Economic Development* (1986, winner of the Ohira Masayoshi Memorial Prize), and *An Introduction to the South Korean Economy* (1996), among many dozens of others.

ABOUT THE TRANSLATOR

Robert D. Eldridge was born in the United States in 1968 and received his Ph.D. in political science from the Graduate School of Law, Kobe University, in 1999, specializing in Japanese Political and Diplomatic History. After becoming a tenured associate professor at the Graduate School of International Public Policy, Osaka University, he joined the U.S. Department of Defense where he served as the deputy assistant chief of staff, Marine Corps Installations Pacific, in Okinawa, Japan. He is the author, editor, contributor, and translator of more than 100 books, including several published by Lexington Books, including *Japan's Backroom Politics:*

Factions in a Multiparty Age (2013), *The Prime Ministers of Postwar Japan, 1945–1995: Their Lives and Times* (2016), and *Changing Security Policies in Postwar Japan: The Political Biography of Japanese Defense Minister Sakata Michita* (2017), and *Japan as an Immigration Nation: Demographic Change, Economic Necessity, and the Human Community Concept* (2020).

www.ingramcontent.com/pod-product-compliance
Lightning Source LLC
Chambersburg PA
CBHW050656280326
41932CB00015B/2932